Harvey Minasian MS (London), FRCS, is a recently retired consultant surgeon. His practice was based in central London, UK. A graduate of The Royal London Hospital, University of London, he has always had an interest in inspiring and encouraging young people to take an interest in science and explore the subject.

A Flyby Journey Through Time

HARVEY MINASIAN

Illustrations by Andrew Pagram

AUSTIN MACAULEY PUBLISHERS™
LONDON · CAMBRIDGE · NEW YORK · SHARJAH

Copyright © Harvey Minasian 2023
Illustrated by Andrew Pagram

The right of **Harvey Minasian** and **Andrew Pagram** to be identified as author and illustrator of this work has been asserted by them in accordance with sections 77 and 78 of the Copyright, Designs and Patents Act 1988.

All rights reserved. No part of this publication may be reproduced, stored in a retrieval system, or transmitted in any form or by any means, electronic, mechanical, photocopying, recording, or otherwise, without the prior permission of the publishers.

Any person who commits any unauthorised act in relation to this publication may be liable to criminal prosecution and civil claims for damages.

A CIP catalogue record for this title is available from the British Library.

ISBN 9781035802494 (Paperback)
ISBN 9781035802500 (ePub e-book)

www.austinmacauley.com

First Published 2023
Austin Macauley Publishers Ltd®
1 Canada Square
Canary Wharf
London
E14 5AA

Dedicated to all young people, including my grandchildren; Lauren, Katie, Brodie and Charlie; who may go on to become scientists.

I would like to thank my family, especially my wife Maggie and my brother Darwin.

Table of Content

Preface	8
Chapter 1: At the Beginning	10
Chapter 2: Much Later	23
Chapter 3: Life	31
Chapter 4: Multicellular Organisms	35
Chapter 5: Humans	40
Chapter 6: Modern Humans	45
Chapter 7: Humans Today and the Near Future	53
Chapter 8: The Far Future	58

Preface

Hello. I hope you will find this short book enjoyable, easy to read and understand. I also hope that at the end of it you will be a little more knowledgeable and wiser. The main purpose of this short book is for you to find out if science interests you or will do after you have read the whole book. The intention is not to overwhelm and saturate you with excessive facts and information. It is a brief "flyby" over the important events from the time when our universe came into existence up to the present day and a little into the future. I have had to use some scientific and other technical words with which you may not be familiar. These, together with important topics, are **bold typed** for you to look up – maybe on the internet and study them further if you wished. Don't forget your parents, teachers and friends are there for you to ask lots of questions and discuss things with them.

Journey's start

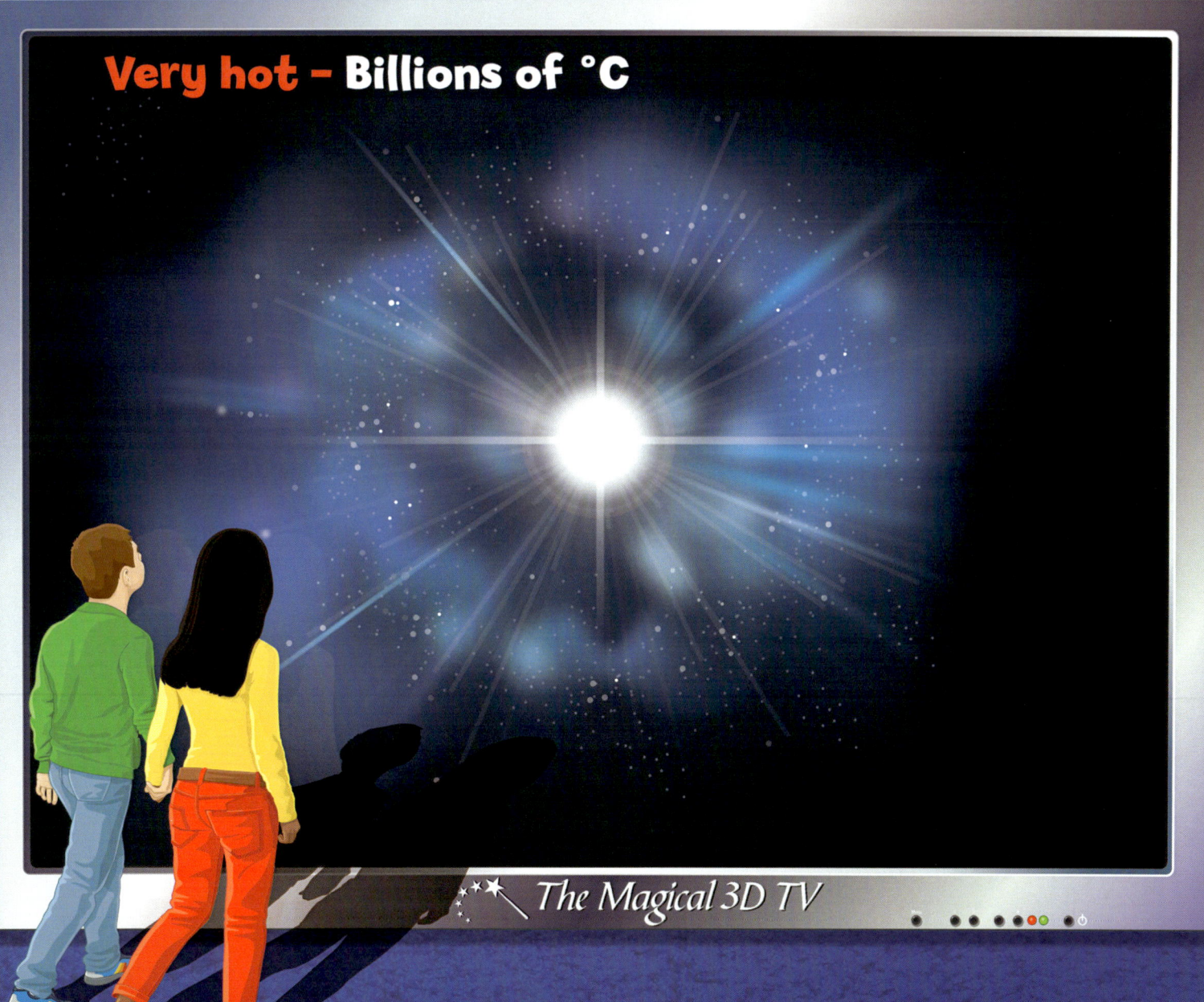

Chapter 1
At the Beginning

Just imagine how incredible it would be, if you were indestructible, and had a gigantic magical three-dimensional TV through which you could look at things that had happened in the past. Even more incredible, you would be able to jump into the screen and flyby whenever you wanted a closer look, but always jump out again into the safety of your home if you were scared, wanted a snack, were fed up or just bored. You would only be able to observe things, but never touch or change anything. Well, let us assume that you were indestructible and had such an amazing set up. The information about the things you will see and experience in your journey through the magical TV screen were brought together by our clever scientists, historians and many others. These clever people have studied, investigated and researched extensively and have come up with the things you will be experiencing. Most of them are accurate and factual, others are best guesses and theories which may become fact later, changed or be discarded, as more and more scientists study them. What you will see is the best they have come up with so far. Not all scientists agree on the details of what happened in the past or know exactly what happened – they are aware of how little they know and all they can do is to guess and theorise – but don't worry, your experience in reading this book together with the magical TV screen and most importantly your imagination should, nevertheless, be useful and hopefully fun. You can always take a break, jump out of that magical screen to ask questions and investigate further what you have seen and learnt.

Let us start at the very beginning – when there was nothing anywhere at all. Even time hadn't started and there was no space – a bit hard to imagine – don't worry if you can't just now, most people can't either. Maybe think of a tiny grain of sand that you can't always see, in the middle of nothingness or nowhere. At this point, you can jump into the screen, but there won't be anything there as space had not been created as yet – so best not to. If you do jump in, jump out again quickly before this miniscule and invisible sand grain that isn't really anything suddenly explodes and expands with an unimaginable force, creating and going on to eventually form everything, (including space) we can see, measure or are aware of today – our **universe**. This **Big Bang** also created many things which we cannot perceive today but may discover in the future. Space, stars like our sun, **galaxies** (huge collection of stars), enormous clumps of very hot gasses and particle dust called **nebulae**, where stars are formed – a sort of star nursery, as well as the beginning of time are examples of what resulted from this Big Bang to make up our universe. It is so strange that this nothingness suddenly becomes everything. This may be difficult to understand, but you have your precious limitless imagination – you can imagine anything you like. You will come to understand a little more of it when you are older, especially if you become a scientist. As we get more information, our understanding of past events changes. For example, recent information sent back from space by the **Hubble** telescope may suggest that maybe there was something before the Big Bang – maybe, a vast ocean of energy in which that little speck of "sand" appeared and then inflated (expanded) as the Big Bang to create space and matter. It is hoped that the recently launched **James Webb Space Telescope**, an improved and updated version of the Hubble, will look further back in time, sending us vital information; something to look forward to.

This Big Bang happened a very, very long time ago. Not a hundred years, a thousand years, a million years or a thousand million years (which is a billion years) but as long as 13.8 billion years ago. We know this, because following the Big Bang, all that came to exist including stars and galaxies, which formed around 300 million years after the Big Bang, have been moving outwards and expanding at enormous speeds. They are accelerating which means their speed is continually increasing. Scientists have measured these speeds and distances and with clever mathematics have estimated the age of the universe, when it all started, by rewinding the events, like you would rewind a recorded TV programme.

Let us jump into the stuff that resulted moments after the ginormous Big Bang, to have a better look. This is an extremely hot place, trillions of degrees centigrade (°C). Good thing you are indestructible, otherwise you would vaporise instantly. It does cool down as the stuff forming the universe expands. In there you will find countless trillions of two main basic ingredients that we know of today:

1. Miniscule extremely fast-moving, energy-carrying particles, so small that billions of them can pass through you without you noticing them. These are referred

11

to as **subatomic particles** – meaning they are smaller than **atoms** (you will come across atoms in the next paragraph).

2.   Energy-carrying **waves** which scientists call **electro-magnetic waves** or **electro-magnetic radiation – EMR** for short or refer to them, simply, as **light**.

Both travel and whizz around in their surrounding space or field (**electro-magnetic field**) at a variety of extremely high speeds, limited to and not exceeding, the **speed of light** when it is travelling through "empty" space (**vacuum**). This speed is exactly 299,792.458 kilometres or 186,282.397 miles every second. Easier to remember approximately 300,000 kilometres or 186,000 miles every second. That would mean travelling to the moon and back in about 1.51 seconds.

There are different kinds of these miniscule subatomic particles, carrying a variety of energy levels, determined by, for example, their spin. They have the ability to react with one another to change their form and properties. The subatomic particles which cannot be split to any smaller parts are referred to as **elementary particles**. Scientists have given these particles various names. Examples are **quarks** and **electrons**. A fraction of a second after the Big Bang, three of these quarks fused together with very strong forces, to form larger particles that we call **neutrons** and **protons**. A proton is very similar to a neutron, but it carries a positive **electrical charge** and has a very slightly lower **mass**. Scientists have calculated that about three minutes after the Big Bang, the ever-expanding universe cooled enough for neutrons and protons to come together, but about 400,000 years had to pass for the universe to cool sufficiently for electrons, which carry a negative electrical charge, to be trapped and added to the protons and neutrons to form the very first **atoms**, the simplest of which was made up of a single proton and a single electron. We have named this atom **hydrogen**, which to this day remains the most abundant atom (73%) in the known universe, mostly in the form of gas. As time went on more protons, neutrons and electrons were added to the hydrogen atom to make other atoms with different energy carrying levels and properties. This process is called **nuclear fusion**. Examples are the addition of another proton, two neutrons and an electron to the hydrogen atom to make what we have called **helium** (He). This is the gas used to fill balloons in parties, to make them float in air. Helium is the second most abundant atom (25%) in the universe and was probably formed seconds after the formation of hydrogen. However, it took hundreds of thousands of years for the hydrogen and helium atoms to become stable in the form we know today. Scientists think it took much longer, up to billions of years for the expanding universe to cool enough to allow the further addition of protons, neutrons and electrons to the helium atom to produce the remaining 2% of the atoms, in the universe. All these atoms, of course, were heavier or more accurately had a greater mass than helium. Mass is not quite the same thing as weight as measured on this Earth. Mass of an object is always the same, but its weight depends on where it is located in the universe, and to what forces it is subjected, for example gravity. Examples of atoms familiar to us are **carbon** (C), **nitrogen** (N), **oxygen** (O), **aluminium** (Al), **silicon** (Si), **iron** (Fe) and still, more massive ones, like **silver** (Ag), **gold** (Au) and **lead** (Pb). Huge amounts of energy were needed and were used up to create these new atoms, especially for the assembly of atoms that were "heavier" (had a greater mass) than iron with the greatest number of neutrons and protons. The energy came from within stars and their transformations during their life cycle. This included the relatively rare but violent event of a **supernova** when a super massive star comes to the end of its life and explodes with an unimaginably enormous force, providing the energy for the production of the atoms heavier than iron. There are 94 different naturally occurring atoms distributed throughout everything in our universe, which includes everything on Earth, in all the plants, animals and us. You could say we are all made of stardust.

Each atom has a central part called the **nucleus**, which is made up of the neutrons and protons, (held together by a very strong force) around which there is a cloud of much, much smaller and hugely distant electrons. All these atoms in the universe differ from one another only in the number of protons, neutrons and electrons they have. The basic ingredients in all of them are the same. In Greek, the word "atom" which means something that can no longer be divided into smaller pieces was coined before we knew that even smaller (subatomic) particles existed and came together to form the atoms. Nevertheless, at our level of understanding and for simplicity, we can consider atoms to be the basic building blocks of our universe. A substance that is made entirely of the same type of atoms is called an **element** or more accurately a **chemical element**. Elements are given the same name as the atoms from which they are made and are listed in order of their mass ("heaviness") in a table, called the **periodic table** which you may have come across at school. If you get a chance to look at this table, you may see up to 118 elements listed. This is because 94 elements are naturally occurring and the rest, 24 elements have been made by us in our laboratories. Elements can exist in different states. They can be solid, liquid or gas, depending on various conditions like temperature and pressure.

In your flyby you will also be bombarded with the energy carrying electro-magnetic waves which are the other known ingredient of the universe. It is easy to imagine particles, however minute they may be, but it is more difficult to imagine waves you cannot see or touch. To make it easier for you to understand waves, imagine a pond, with still water which we can liken to the space or the field where the waves can appear and travel. Then imagine dropping a stone in the middle of the pond disturbing and adding energy to the water. You will see circular waves (ripples) spreading outwards, towards the edge of the pond, hitting the edges and being reflected. It is interesting that the moment the stone hits the water, the wave created is travelling at a constant speed. It didn't have to accelerate (gather speed – get faster and faster) from a stationary position to reach that speed. The electro-magnetic waves in the space (or their field) behave in much the same way. Even more amazing is that some energy-carrying electro-magnetic waves can also behave like minute sub-atomic elementary particles and these particles can shape-shift and behave like electro-magnetic waves. They can jump in or out of being either, as far as their behaviour is concerned, and we may consider them as "one and the same". Scientists have found this out using experiments, but these experiments have their limitations. This dual particle or wave behaviour (called **wave-particle duality**) is difficult to understand, or visualise, even by some well-established scientists, so you don't have to worry about it too much. To make things even more complicated and confusing, recent findings show that much larger sub-atomic particles such as protons can also have wave-like characteristics. These electro-magnetic waves are always on the move and travel at the speed of light but have different shapes and carry different amounts of energy. The range of these waves is collectively referred to as **the electro-magnetic spectrum (EM spectrum)**. They whizz around and interact with other waves and particles. The energy of an electro-magnetic wave is carried in discrete amounts called **quanta** (singular **quantum**), a bit like pockets or bundles. Each quantum of energy they carry is referred to as a **photon**, which can behave either as a particle or a wave. Some people use the term photon and electro-magnetic wave to mean the same thing. The energy depends on how squashed together the wave peaks are (**frequency** of the wave – expressed in **hertz** units, **Hz** for short) and how tall the wave is (**amplitude** of the wave). The more squashed (high frequency) and taller the wave (high amplitude) the greater the energy they carry. Their properties and effects they have when they hit other waves, particles or objects, is accordingly different. The electro-magnetic waves with the highest frequency and energy are called gamma rays. The waves with the lowest frequency are the radio waves. The light we see is made of electro-magnetic rays with frequencies that sit somewhere in the middle of the electro-magnetic spectrum. When millions of them hit the cells in the retina, at the back of our eyes, they have the ability to stimulate these cells making our brains perceive it as visible light. Other electro-magnetic waves, with different shapes, energy levels and properties, such as radio waves have no effect on our retina, and we don't see them. X-rays are another example of electro-magnetic waves, which have the ability to go through tissues like skin and muscle and are used in medicine to take pictures inside the body. Some high energy electro-magnetic waves, if numerous enough, are harmful to our body cells and can cause damage or even death. Note that some scientists use the word light to refer to the whole of the electro-magnetic spectrum, while others use it to refer only to that part of the spectrum that our eyes can see – maybe in this case, for clarity, it would be best to use the term visible light. Looking at, studying and analysing some electro-magnetic waves coming from space can tell the scientists a great deal. This is because all atoms have some heat energy stored in them and emit (give off) these waves, with each type of atom having its unique wave frequency just like a signature or a footprint. Scientists can then map out the nature of the types of atoms, elements or molecules that make up the objects and gasses in deep space. They have confirmed that all the various types of atoms are exclusively the same as the ones that make up our planet and everything in it, including us. Currently, huge telescopes are being built in South Africa and Australia to detect even the very weak radio waves which have travelled from the outer boundaries of our observable universe. Remember that all the electro-magnetic waves we detect would have had to travel (at speed of light) over billions of years to reach us – so what we see now in deep space is that which existed or happened billions of years ago!

Within the expanding universe, there are also different entities at play which we see as having the effect of pulling particles or clumps of particles, such as objects, together or sometimes repelling them from one another. They behave like **forces** and for simplicity we can regard them as such. There are four of these in nature. An example is **gravity**, something we still know very little about or understand which behaves as an attracting force and we see as pulling particles or objects together. It is by far the star of the show in the ever-changing and expanding universe. Gravity is strongest near massive objects. In fact, the closer you are and the bigger the object, the greater this pulling together effect would be. **Magnetism or electro-magnetism** (where opposing poles pull together and similar poles repel one another) is another example of a force active in the universe.

As you fly through the expanding universe looking through your magical microscope, you will see that in time, maybe on planets orbiting their suns or on large rocks (**asteroids**), some of these different types of atoms and elements combine together to form clumps of larger particles we call **molecules**. An example is water, which is a combination of two atoms of hydrogen and one of oxygen. Another example is the combination of oxygen with the element silicon to form the main body of most rocks so abundant on the surface of our planet. Different molecules clump together to form what are referred to as **compounds**. Example of compounds are **proteins** which are made up of **amino acid** molecules, containing the atoms carbon (C), hydrogen (H), oxygen (O) and nitrogen (N). Substances containing carbon are called **organic compounds**. They are present in every living tissue and life would not be possible without the presence of carbon – another star of our show.

Particles and Atoms

Quarks and electrons are examples of subatomic particles. Electrons always carry a negative charge.

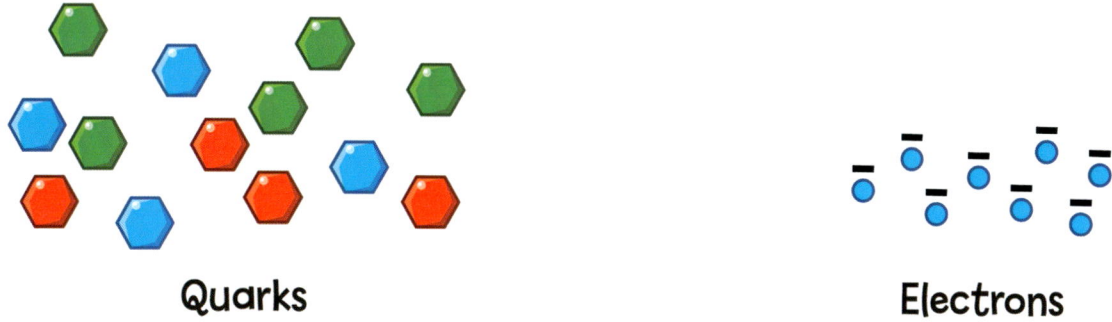

Quarks are a friendly lot – they don't hang around by themselves. They are always with other quarks. 3 of them get together and are held by a very strong force to form a neutron. Add a positive electric charge and a proton is created, which has a very slightly lower mass than a neutron.

When an electron is trapped in orbit around a single proton a hydrogen atom is born. It is the simplest and commonest atom in the universe.

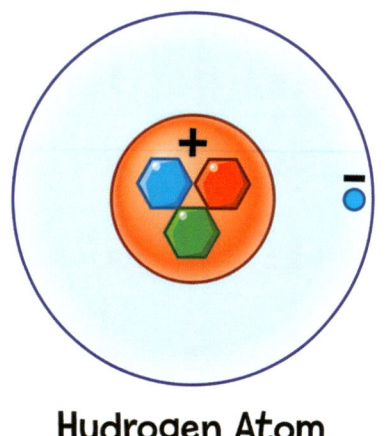

When another proton, 2 neutrons and another electron are added to the hydrogen atom a helium atom is formed – the second commonest atom in the universe.

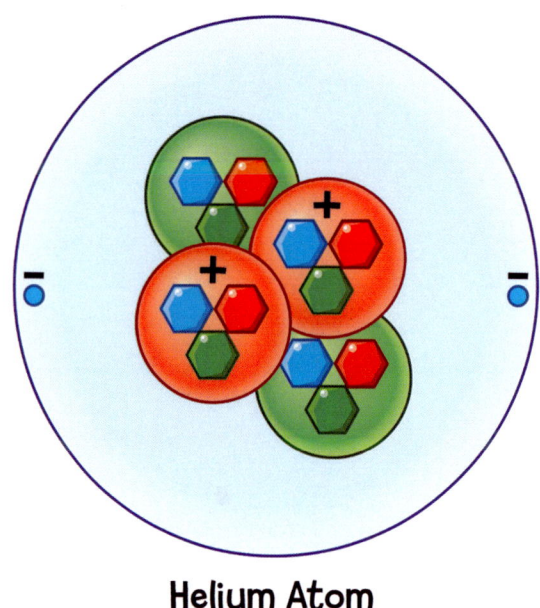

Helium Atom

Further assembly of protons, neutrons and electrons result in a variety of larger and more massive atoms. Examples are:

A carbon atom which has	6 protons 6 neutrons and 6 electrons
A nitrogen atom which has	7 protons 7 neutrons and 7 electrons
An oxygen atom which has	8 protons 8 neutrons and 8 electrons
An aluminium atom which has	13 protons 14 neutrons and 13 electrons
A silicon atom which has	14 protons 14 neutrons and 14 electrons
An iron atom which has	26 protons 30 neutrons and 26 electrons
A silver atom which has	47 protons 61 neutrons and 47 electrons
A gold atom which has	79 protons 118 neutrons and 79 electrons
A lead atom which has	82 protons 125 neutrons and 82 electrons

The basic ingredients of all the atoms in our universe are the same – made of protons, neutrons and electrons

Molecules and Compounds

Atoms join up to make molecules, for example water which is a simple molecule consisting of 2 atoms of hydrogen and 1 atom of oxygen – formula H_2O. Depending on how the molecules are arranged, water can exist in gas, liquid or solid states which is so important for living organisms.

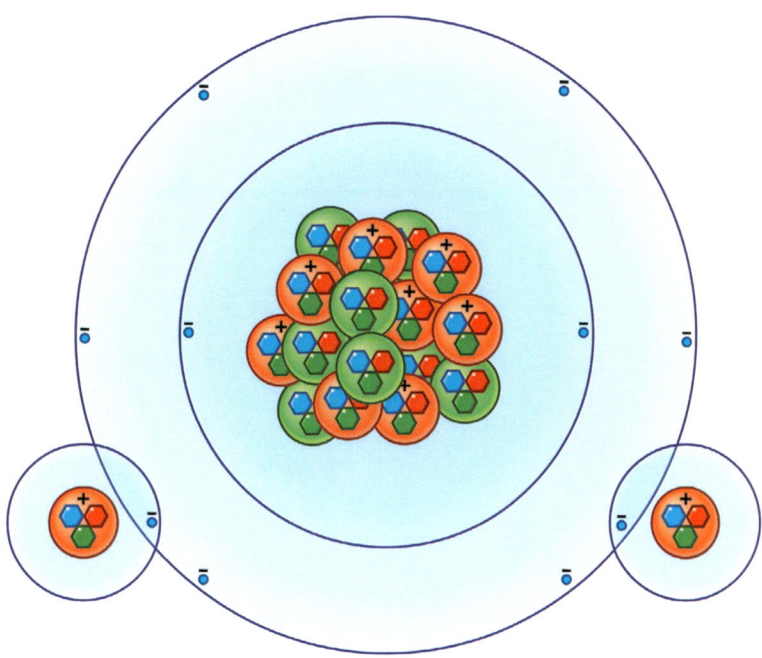

Water Molecule

Albumin, which is a protein, abundant in our blood stream has 388 atoms.

Some molecules can be enormous, such as our DNA (Deoxyribonucleic Acid), carried in the nucleus of our cells. A single strand of DNA molecule – a chromosome – can have around 10 billion atoms.

What a molecule of DNA looks like under enormous magnification, using an electron microscope.

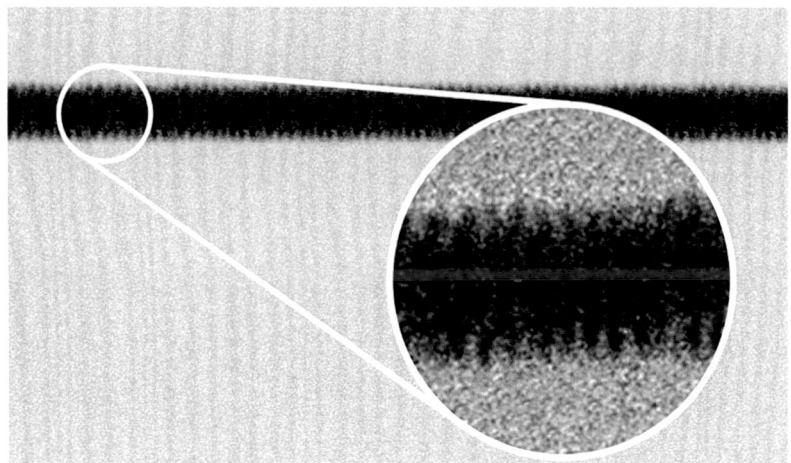

The Electro-magnetic Spectrum

This covers a huge range of electro-magnetic wave frequencies. At one end of the spectrum are the radio waves with the lowest frequency and energy and at the other end are the gamma (γ) rays with the highest frequency and energy levels.

In between are the microwaves, infrared waves, visible light waves, ultraviolet waves and X-rays.

They have different properties and use

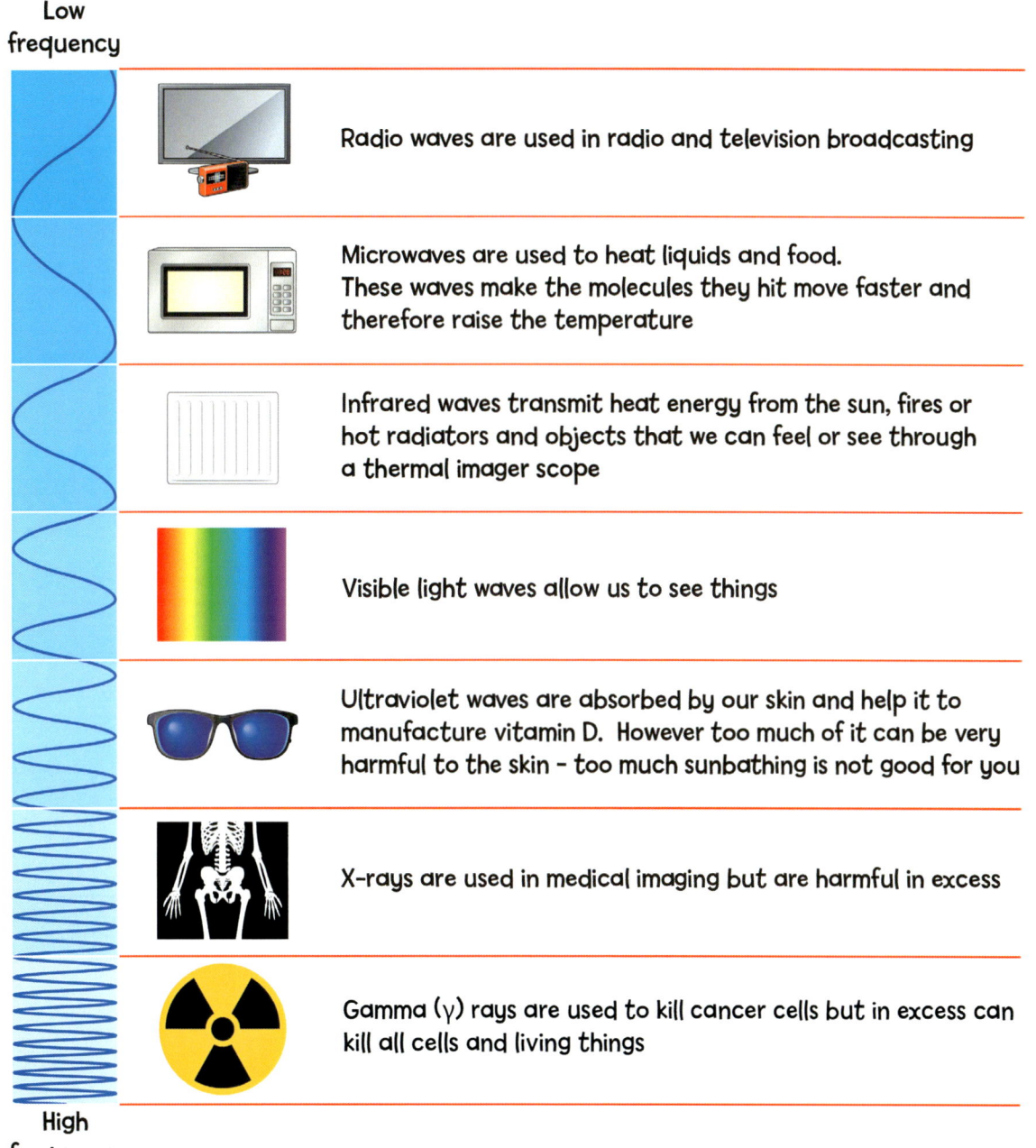

About visible light waves:

Over millions of years some of the retinal cells at the back of eyes have evolved to be stimulated by the visible light wave segment of the electro-magnetic spectrum. These cells pass electrical signals on to the brain, which are perceived as light. This segment roughly sits in the middle of the spectrum. Our and some animals' retinal cells have become even more specialised to further analyse the frequencies of the waves in the white light segment and we perceive these as the 7 colours of the rainbow (or their combination). The colours are: Red, Yellow, Orange, Green, Blue, Indigo and Violet.

To make it easy for you to remember the order of these colours you can use the phrase (an mnemonic or memory aid):

Richard Of York Gave Battle In Vain

Chapter 2
Much Later

9.5 billion years have now passed – it is 4.5 billion years ago. The universe is still expanding and has got a lot bigger and cooler. That magical thing, gravity has played its cards. Particles, atoms and elements, molecules and compounds have come together to form enormous bodies of matter and objects in the universe. Most dramatic are stars, hot bodies that radiate lots of electro-magnetic waves and subatomic particles. The only reason we can see them is because they also emit a huge number of the type of electro-magnetic waves which we are able to perceive as visible light. The majority of stars are made of hydrogen and helium, like our own sun and are grouped together as galaxies. There are two trillion galaxies each hoarding hundreds of billions of stars. There are enormous distances between the stars and galaxies – millions or billions of **light years**. A light year is a measure of distance – it is the distance that light travels in the given number of years. Nearly all the universe is "empty" space, or at least that is how we see it. Scientists have given such names as **dark matter** and **dark energy** to these "empty" spaces which apparently make up 95% of the universe. You don't need to bother with these for now, as we are not really equipped with the senses to directly detect, perceive and understand them. Maybe for our current knowledge of understanding, we should rename dark matter to "doesn't matter"!

The universe is a highly active and complex place. New stars and the planets that orbit them are being born in nebulae – in giant clumps of gases and particle dusts. Old stars are dying as they run out of fuel, explode and collapse in on themselves under the effects of gravity. Some of these form relatively small but super massive and dense bodies that generate gravitational effects enormous enough to stop even electro-magnetic waves escaping. To us they appear dark and are called **black holes**. Just a reminder that all the types of particles, atoms and electro-magnetic waves that are distributed in the universe are the same that we find here on Earth. Our planet is a tiny bit of the universe. The laws of physics and chemistry we know of and can apply to our everyday life also apply to what goes on in our universe, except when we look at exceedingly small things like atoms or subatomic particles as in **quantum physics** and very big things like super massive objects in deep space, for example black holes. So far, no one has been able to find laws that would apply to everything, thus unifying them, not even **Albert Einstein** (who lived from 1879 to 1955), one of the greatest physicists and mathematicians of all time. He gave us the famous formula, $E=mc^2$ relating energy (E) to mass of a body at rest (m) and speed of light (c). Maybe, one day you will be the one to discover such unification laws. Imagine the glory and fame if you succeed.

Flyby through the galaxies and clouds of dust, dodging the hot stars and black holes in the middle of galaxies and home in on the space around our sun – the **solar system**. The sun is a giant fireball made of hydrogen and helium brought together by the effect of gravity. Its energy and heat in the form of electro-magnetic waves, atoms and subatomic particles that it throws outwards into space, comes from the conversion of hydrogen into helium. Large clumps of hot rocky debris are swirling round the sun, colliding into one another with horrendous force. That magical gravity is at it again, not only bringing together more and more of the rocky and icy objects but also keeping them in orbit round the young sun. Eventually, in time, over millions of years, the eight planets and their moons form. Our Earth is one of them. Our home is born. It is the third furthest planet away from the sun. As would be expected its surface gets less heat from the sun when compared to the closest planet, Mercury and far more heat than the planet Neptune which is the furthest away from the sun. This makes the conditions on these planets so different from one another. The distances between the sun and the planets are huge compared to their sizes, just like the way it is for the stars in the universe. Go and visit the planets and see it for yourself. Take care; our planet is a very hot and hostile place with erupting volcanoes and no real atmosphere as we know it today.

Over the next 500 million (half of a billion) years our planet gradually cools. Its surface forms a crust, but not a perfect one. It has lots of cracks in it, separating the crust into irregular plates. These are the present day **tectonic plates.** They have been moving rather slowly crashing into one another to bulge up to form mountains (such as the Himalayas in Asia and the Alps in Europe) or diving under one another (**subduction**) causing huge earthquakes and volcanic eruptions. All these have resulted in a crust surface full of depressions and elevations. The slow movements of the tectonic plates continue to this day causing earthquakes and volcanic activity. Interestingly, the Himalayan mountains, which include Mount

Everest – the highest mountain in the world – are still rising by 10 cm every year. In 2005, a huge earthquake in the west Himalayas in northern Pakistan resulted in the elevation of the surrounding land by a staggering 5 metres.

In time water, which had been ejected as steam from volcanoes and also brought to Earth via countless billions of ice-containing comet strikes, filled the depressions and troughs on the surface of Earth's crusts to form the oceans and the seas. Under the cooling crust it is still extremely hot – the rocks and other materials are molten – in liquid form. In the centre of the Earth is a large reservoir of molten iron (Fe). The Earth spins in an anti-clockwise direction, a lingering "gift" from the days of the Big Bang and, yes, the star of our show, gravity. If you have jumped in to see what is going on, don't worry about this spin, you won't be left behind, good old gravity will take you with it. The spin of the Earth and the movements of the molten metals, mostly iron, in the core of the Earth trigger a **magnetic field** around the Earth, as though a giant magnet was placed across the Earth from north to south. This is very fortunate, as this magnetic field, which is like a cocoon surrounding our planet, is still here today acting like a shield, protects life forms from harmful electro-magnetic waves and particles radiating from the sun, that rush, at the speed of light, to hit our planet.

Nebula – a giant mass of dust and gasses, mostly hydrogen and helium – a sort of nursery for stars, where they are born under the influence of gravity and go through their life cycle. This is an image of the Orion nebula which is within The Milky Way galaxy where our planet is. It is visible from most parts of the world from November to February.

The Orion nebula

Clumps of rocky and icy objects collide and eventually, under the effects of gravity come together to form much larger masses – our planet in one of them.

Formation of the Solar System

The developing **primitive Earth** is a hot object with a molten core packed with energy – a legacy from the time of the Big Bang.

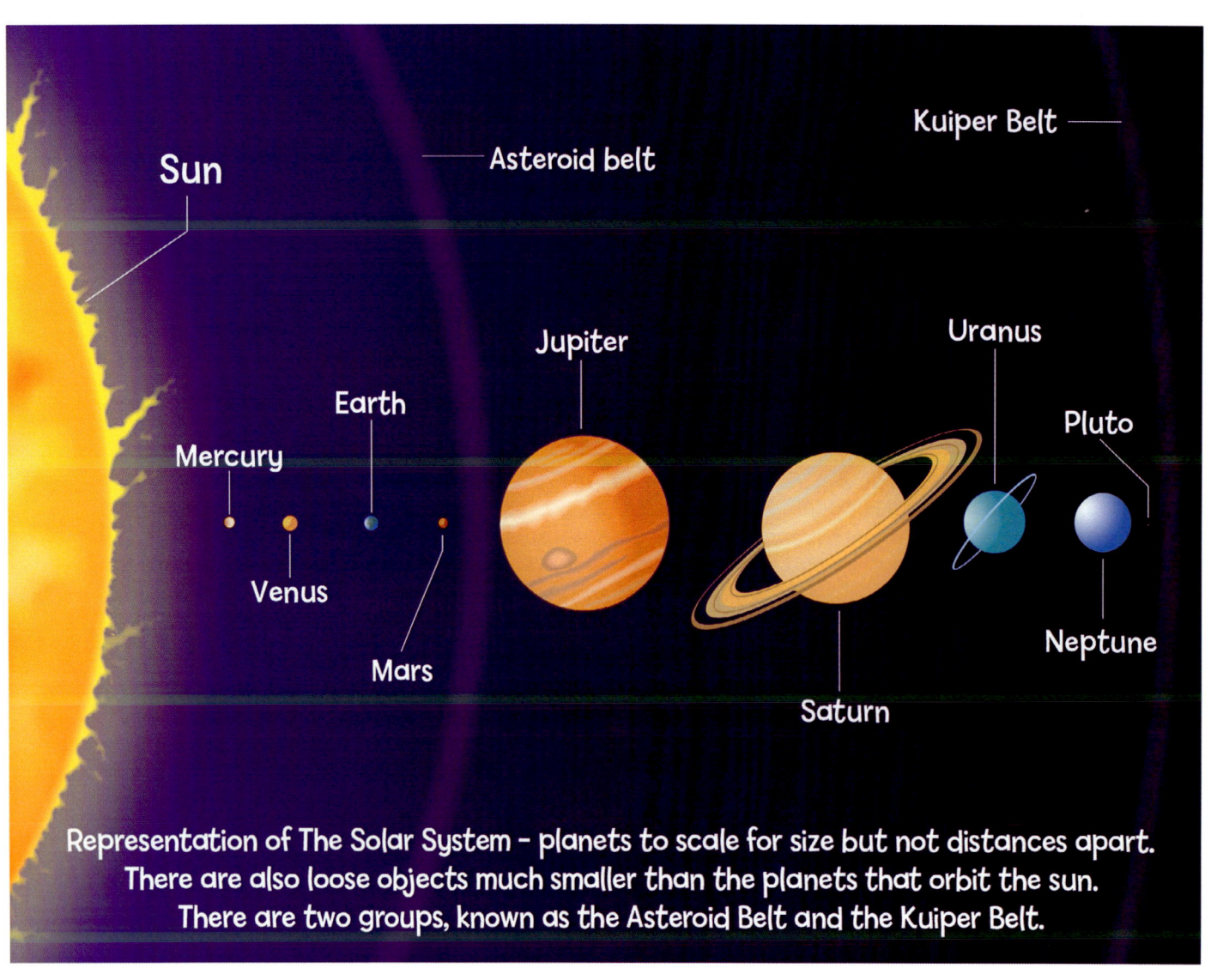

Representation of The Solar System – planets to scale for size but not distances apart. There are also loose objects much smaller than the planets that orbit the sun. There are two groups, known as the Asteroid Belt and the Kuiper Belt.

As our planet cools, its surface forms a crust, broken up into what we call the Tectonic plates.

Current day tectonic plates and their main direction of movement. About 230 million years ago when the dinosaurs roamed the Earth, these plates were arranged such that all the land masses above water level were stuck together as one lump called the Pangea.

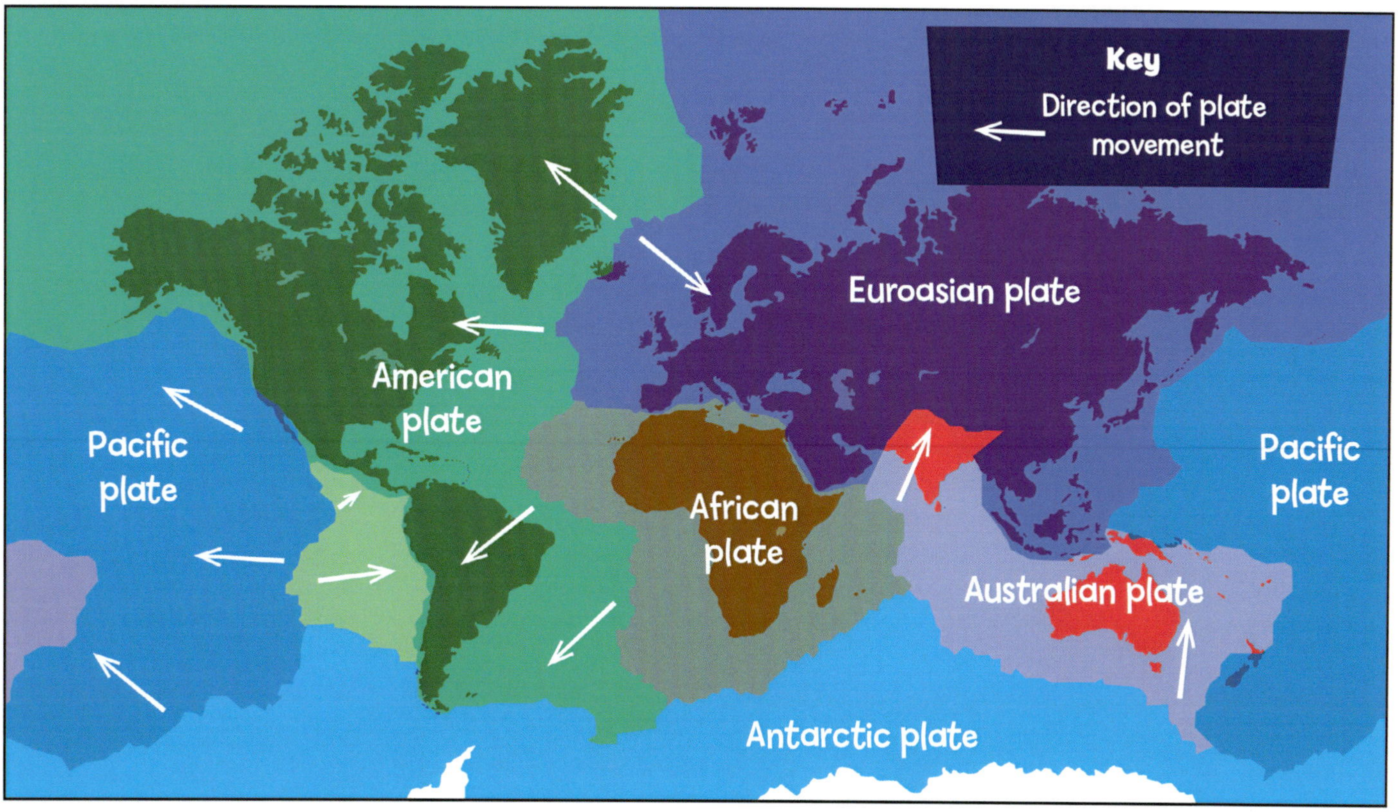

Tectonic plates are always on the move at speeds of 6 to 10 centimetres per year. They crash into or dive under one another (subduction) to form mountains and volcanoes. Most earthquakes occur along or close to the junctions of these plates.

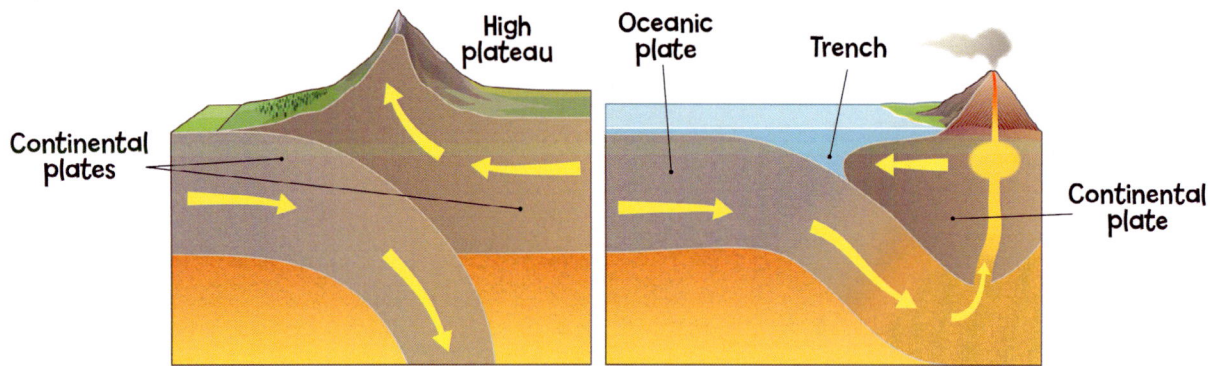

The Himalayan Mountain Range and the Tibetan Plateau as shown in this aerial view, formed when the Indo-Australian plate from the south and the Eurasian plate in the north collided, around 50 million years ago.

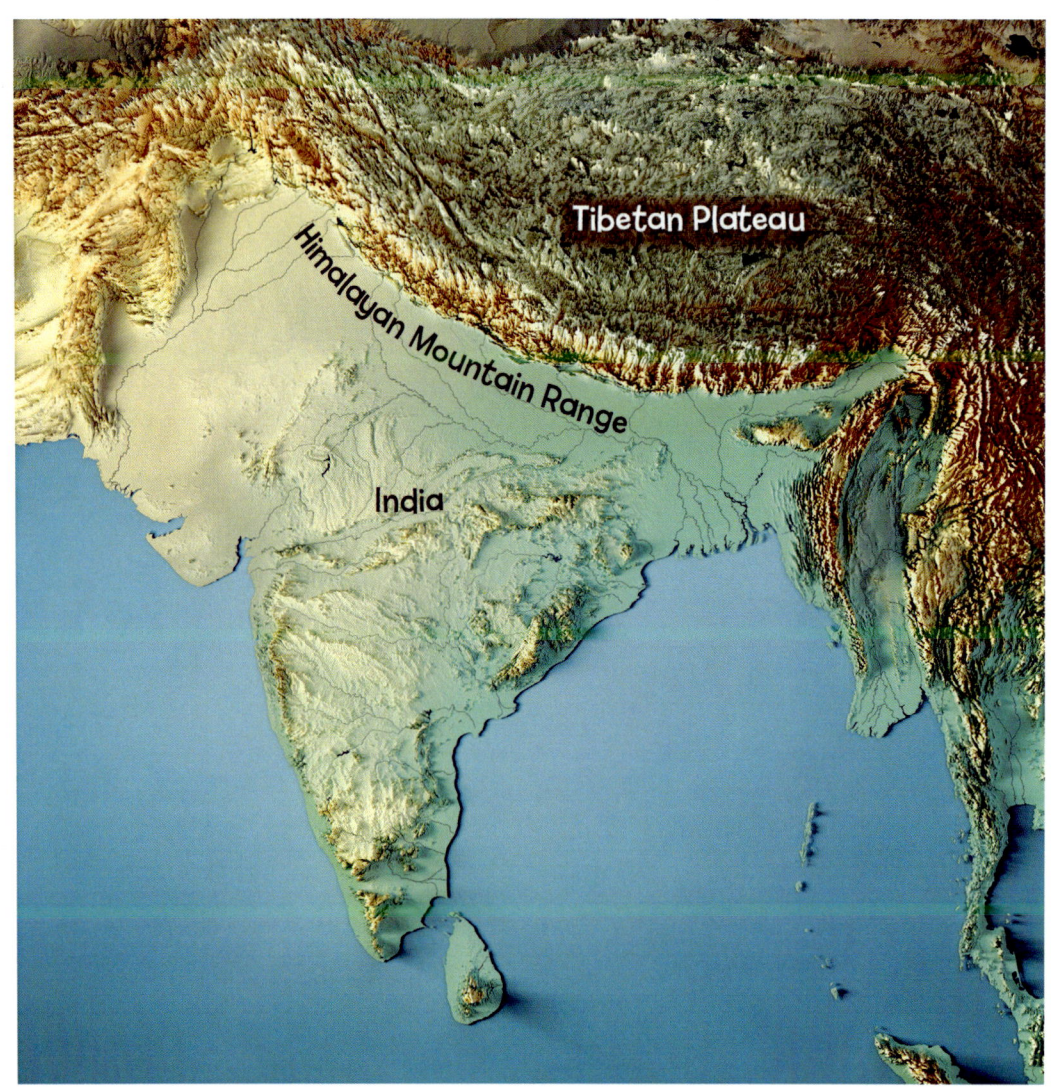

Chapter 3
Life

Another 500 million (half of a billion) years has passed. It is 4 billion years ago. Our planet is still a hostile, unfriendly place, with volcanoes spewing out lava. Many rocky and icy clumps (**meteors**, asteroids, and **comets**) from space are hitting the Earth and exploding. There was, probably, a kind of atmosphere mostly made of gases thrown up by the volcanoes. Around this time, most likely, in a watery environment something quite amazing happened – **life** started. No one is quite sure where and how this came about, but we can have a good guess. Remember the various types of atoms, elements and molecules you read about – these were constantly combining and reacting with one another. There must have been billions and billions of such reactions every second. It is therefore not surprising that at some stage, by chance, a combination of such chemicals resulted in an incredibly unique molecule, that was so designed to have the ability to make copies of itself – to **replicate**, using the molecules floating round it, in a watery environment. **DNA** (which stands for Deoxyribonucleic acid), which you may have heard of, present in every living cell, is such a molecule made up of unique molecules collectively known as **nucleotides**, which we can regard as the building blocks of life. It is quite likely that the first replicator molecule had a similar structure to that of the spiral DNA we know today. The copies were not always perfect, and had some mistakes in them, but most copies retained the ability to replicate, but again with some mistakes in the copies. It is these mistakes and resulting imperfect (faulty) replications which will prove to be so fundamentally important in the production of the diversity (variety) of life forms we see today, ranging from viruses to simple plants to giants like dinosaurs and on to super intelligent animals like us humans. Without these mistakes life would be limited to a single form or not exist at all.

This chance ability of this complex molecule to replicate seems not only to have persisted (stayed, lived on) but also to have become an unstoppable event. It's goal, present to this day, was to **replicate, survive and spread at the expense of all else**. These reactions and replications carried on over the next 500 million years or so – producing more and more complex molecules (compounds) with the ability to replicate. Viruses are examples of these, some remaining hardly changed to this day. As these reactions progressed, far more complex molecular structures were formed and assembled to form what we refer to as **single cell organisms**, able to replicate just like their predecessors. Scientists think that these chemical reactions may well have taken place in **warm water rock pools**, (where the chemicals would be concentrated), by seashores, hot springs or maybe deep in the oceans, near **volcanic hydrothermal vents**.

Bacteria, some present relatively unchanged to this day, are a good example of single cell organism. An important early one was the blue coloured **Cyanobacteria** (cyan means blue). This spread widely in the oceans and importantly, had the ability to isolate oxygen – which was small and light enough to overcome gravity and escape into the primitive atmosphere. This would prove to be so important for the future as land living organisms would use this oxygen in the atmosphere (air) for their energy needs. For the next 3.5 billion years these single-celled organisms went on replicating and spreading, without any dramatic change to their form.

The first replicating molecules – beginning of life – may have formed in:

Rock pools

Hot springs

A hot spring in Yellowstone National Park in the USA

or hydrothermal vents

Single cell organisms can be miniscule measuring 1-2 micrometres (a micrometre is one thousandth of a millimetre) like the bacteria in intestines of animals, called Escherichia Coli, E. Coli for short.

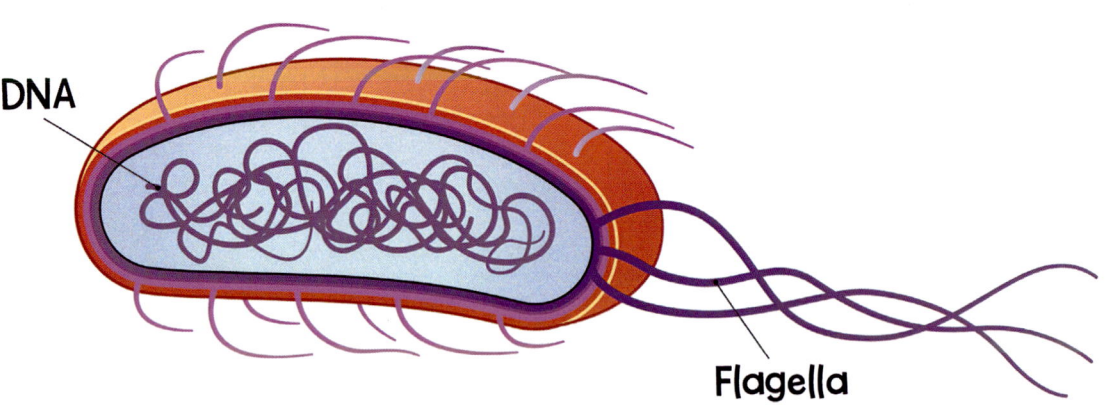

Or they can be large like the seaweed called Caulerpa Taxifolia which can measure up to 30 centimetres.

Chapter 4
Multicellular Organisms

Another 2.5 billion years have now passed. It is now only 1.5 billion years ago. Another amazing but extremely rare event is about to take place. The event was the gobbling up (swallowing – **phagocytosis**) of one single cell organism by another. The cell that was gobbled up became the powerhouse, a sort of factory, able to produce energy for the cell to change, allowing it to become far more active and to go on to form far more complex organisms with many cells working together as one – a **multicellular organism** like us. That gobbled up cell is present, in one form or another, in every plant and animal cell we know of today and is referred to as the **mitochondrion** (plural is mitochondria). Without these, life on Earth would be limited to viruses and single cell organisms. It is interesting that because of the chances of this "gobbling up" event being so infinitely smaller than the chance formation of the first replicating molecule, scientists think that life elsewhere in the universe, if present, is far more likely to be limited to virus-like and single cell organisms only. There are a large variety of plant and animal cells. Overall, their size has not changed much since their appearance 1.5 billion years ago. Big animals like elephants have more of them, compared to smaller animals. Living organisms need energy to survive and flourish. Almost all this energy comes from the sun in the form of sunshine. Plant cells (and some unicellular organisms) have clever chemistry to trap and use this energy. This process is called **photosynthesis**. The trapped energy is passed on to other animals who eat these plants (**herbivores**) and passed on again when they in turn are eaten by meat eating animals (**carnivores**).

Over the next hundreds of millions of years this relentless and persistent replication with the odd mistakes resulted in a great variety of plant and animal forms. These living things were always structured (made up) to interact with and make use of their environment to help their survival. In time they developed specialised groups of cells which had evolved for this purpose. Examples are groups of muscle cells to allow movement; layers of cells (as in the gut) to extract nutrition from food; cells to detect temperature or pressure changes (as in touch sensation) cells to detect the nature of air-born or "in contact" molecules (smell and taste) cells to detect certain sound waves (hearing), and of course to detect certain types of electro-magnetic waves (the ability to react to or see light).

All forms of plant and animal life became dependent on each other for their survival. Any change in one affected the rest – this is what we refer to as an **ecosystem**. The rule of "survive, multiply and spread" was, of course, unchanged. Next time you go for a walk in a woodland in the spring, have a good look at the ground and see the many saplings of various trees, shrubs and vegetation that have taken hold and are competing or "jockeying" for the best sunny positions.

The features of the new animals or plants that came about, were always "add-ons" or sometimes "subtractions" from the ones immediately before. For example, a new animal that emerged and flourished was never a brand-new design and creation, but rather was just the previous or older design, only modified and revised. That is why we share so many features with other animals and plants. The genetic material (DNA) in our cells has very many similarities with those in far less complex animals. We share around 70% of our genes with earthworms and 50% with bananas. Remember this every time you bite into a banana!

The environmental conditions such as weather, temperature and atmosphere were constantly changing due to a variety of reasons, including volcanic activity, meteor strikes, small alterations in the **tilt of our spinning planet**, which brings about the seasons and, even maybe, due to alterations in the Earth's orbit around the sun. These environmental changes resulted in the so called **ice ages and greenhouse periods** when the temperature throughout Earth either falls to cause the expansion of the glaciers from the north and south poles or the temperature rises to result in an ice-free world. There have been at least 5 major ice ages, the last one, probably started around 100 thousand years ago, reached its maximum about 25 thousand years ago and started to decline around 15 thousand years ago. We are now in between the last ice age and a greenhouse period.

Some of these conditions were not suited for the survival of some of the plants and animals. As a result they died out, usually from a shortage of food (vegetation or meat), leaving the plants and animal forms that could use the new environmental conditions to their advantage to adapt and go on to replicate (reproduce) and thrive. This process is referred to as **"Natural selection and the survival of the fittest"** as discovered and described by one of the greatest scientists in history, **Charles Darwin**. A good example is the demise of the dinosaurs. Being so big they could not withstand sudden, dramatic climatic or other changes and died out mostly due to a shortage of food, leaving other smaller animals, such as mammals (our ancestors), to flourish. Would be interesting but sad to flyby during this period, around 65 million years ago, to see how these magnificent creatures died out. To our knowledge, there have been 5 major extinctions of living things, but there have always been survivors and life forms have recovered again, but with many changes to them. We know of these events that took place in the past from the "footprints" such as **fossils** that animals and plants, very kindly, left behind for us to discover today. Scientists have a clever way to tell the age of fossils, using what is known as **Carbon dating** or **Radiocarbon dating.** Remember the great importance of the imperfect copying when replication took place. This imperfect copying process became the key to generating different forms of animals. Without this there would not have been a variety of living things.

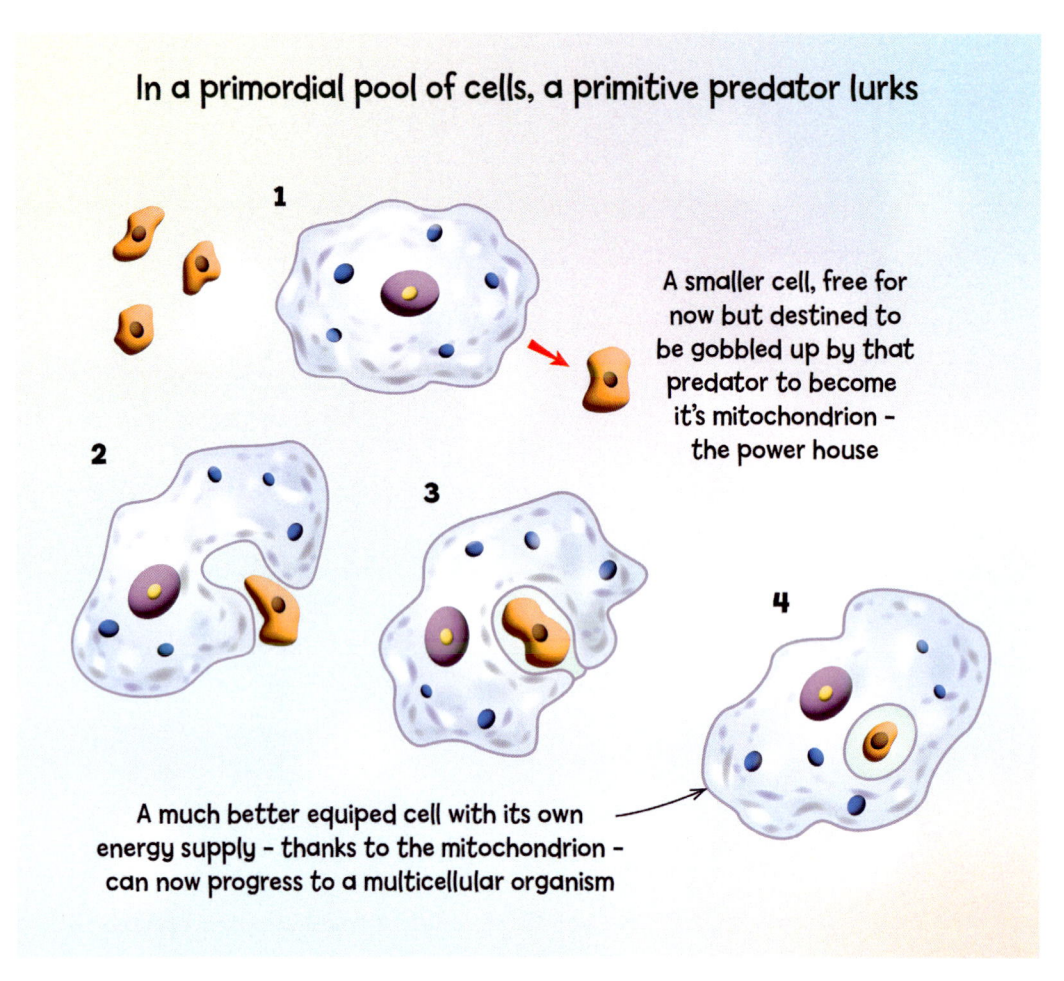

In a primordial pool of cells, a primitive predator lurks

1

A smaller cell, free for now but destined to be gobbled up by that predator to become it's mitochondrion - the power house

2

3

4

A much better equiped cell with its own energy supply - thanks to the mitochondrion - can now progress to a multicellular organism

---

"You are very small"

"Yes, that may be, but my cells are much the same size as yours, and .... your DNA is not much different from mine either"

The last ice age probably started about 100,000 years ago, reached its maximum around 25,000 years ago when the ice sheet may have been up to 4 kilometres thick. In the northern hemisphere it covered a large chunk of Europe, including most of the British Isles – may have even reached London.

To the west, it covered the whole of Canada and northern part of America. The southern hemisphere was far less severely affected.

Chapter 5
Humans

For the next 500 million years or so, life forms (plants and animals), progressed, with huge diversity, some dying out and others flourishing. One group of survivors were the **Primates**, like monkeys (they have a tail) and apes (they don't have a tail). Chimpanzees are apes and are thought to be our closest relatives. Around only 7 million years ago, some apes began to change (evolve) and over the next 2-3 million years became particularly well suited to the environmental conditions of the time. They had the ability to walk on two, rather than four legs as evident from their fossilised footprints. These creatures have been called **Hominids**, our true ancestors who lived in Africa. Carbon dating of their fossilised footprints has shown that they may have left these over 4 million years ago. The most famous fossilised bones are those of a young woman, nicknamed **Lucy** which are 3.2 million years old and that of **Ardi**, which dates back to 4.4 million years. Walking on two legs and also the developing a thumb to grip things were to prove a really big advantage for these Hominids to flourish. These early Hominids changed and evolved to look more and more like us today. For example, they evolved to be more upright rather than hunched. One such group referred to as **Homo Erectus** (means upright man) appeared some 2 million years ago. Changes continued, but the biggest, most dramatic, and most advantageous one, was arguably (at least for that time) the development of a larger brain and finally human intelligence which appeared only around 300,000 years ago. This group are referred to as **Homo Sapiens**, which means wise man.

The urge to travel and explore was a strong feature in Homo Erectus and Homo Sapiens as it is in most of us today. It is, therefore, not surprising that they migrated out of Africa, travelling north. The Homo Sapiens migration was only 200,000 years ago. Do note how late this is in the history of life on our planet, which appeared 4 billion years ago! Homo Sapiens travelled far, normally along shorelines as these were safe and easy places (flat ground) on which to walk. They crossed rivers and seas using their intelligence and ingenuity to build such things as boats to help them. They took advantage of frozen seas in the winter to walk across them. It was not long until they had spread to colonise the whole world. Do make a flyby to see how their intelligence helped them to get around and survive, even in the toughest of conditions. Interestingly, scientists think that outside of Africa, every human being on this planet today can be traced back to and is related to one woman. Scientists know this from DNA tests. You could say that most of us on this planet are related to one another.

Long before the migration of Homo Sapiens, around 1.6 million years ago, Homo Erectus left Africa and travelled north and east. Over the next 1.45 million years, that is around 150,000 years ago, in Europe, they changed to what we call the **Neanderthals**. They co-existed and lived side by side with the Homo Sapiens in Europe until only 25,000 years ago, when they seem to have died out. They were probably just as clever as Homo Sapiens but had a different way of life. They were better suited to live in wooded areas and were unable to survive when the climate in Europe changed and wooded areas were transformed into open land. This is another example of Charles Darwin's "Natural Selection and Survival of the Fittest".

Like most other animal species, Homo Sapiens' behaviour was geared to survival as a group. As would be expected, their priority was to look after their children and those genetically related to them. Living as a group or tribe was safer as they could look out for danger and help one another in a time of need – you may have heard of the expression "there is safety in numbers". In addition, humans, like many other herd animals, were social creatures, preferring to live in groups rather than by themselves. Individuals had differing capabilities and talents. For example, some were predominantly muscular, strong, and good fighters. Some were gifted with higher intelligence and problem-solving skills and some had leadership qualities. Each individual found a useful role to play in the group which benefitted everyone in that group or society. They soon found out that the group fared better if there was a leader (or leaders) to direct them, just as it is today. Sometimes giving excessive power and control to one leader (a **dictator**) caused problems as the wishes of the majority of the people (as in a **democracy**) were not followed. One thing they valued and cherished most was their **freedom** to express themselves freely and do as they wished, rather than be forced to or be told what they can or can't do. This feeling was so strong that many conflicts took place and wars were fought, even to this day, for the right to this liberty. As groups, humans appeared to have developed a need to look up to and worship beings or objects, which they thought were superior with powers they themselves did not or could not have. Maybe this was because during difficult or sad times, they found comfort in communicating with or praying to a higher entity, asking them for help or forgiveness. This included offering them gifts, such as sacrifices, to be rewarded, in return, with better fortunes, for example a good harvest or victory in battle. This was the beginnings of **religion**.

To survive as a group, there were three important things they had to do – get **food and water,** find **shelter** and **reproduce**. Like all other living forms, this urge to replicate and reproduce, (present since that first molecule made a copy of itself), became firmly imprinted or "hardwired" into their brains – something we refer to as **instinct** which you can think of as a sort of behaviour we are born with, rather than learnt, and of which we are not conscious. An interesting example of instinct, present in many of us, is our preference for high calorie food like sugars and fats. Our brains have become conditioned to perceive and feel pleasure every time these high calorie food molecules hit our taste buds. No wonder junk food is so popular and the fast-food industry is doing so well! This instinct was essential when there was a shortage of food, but nowadays when there is no such food shortage in wealthier countries, it has become a problem causing obesity and all the health problems that go with it.

Life on earth evolution timeline

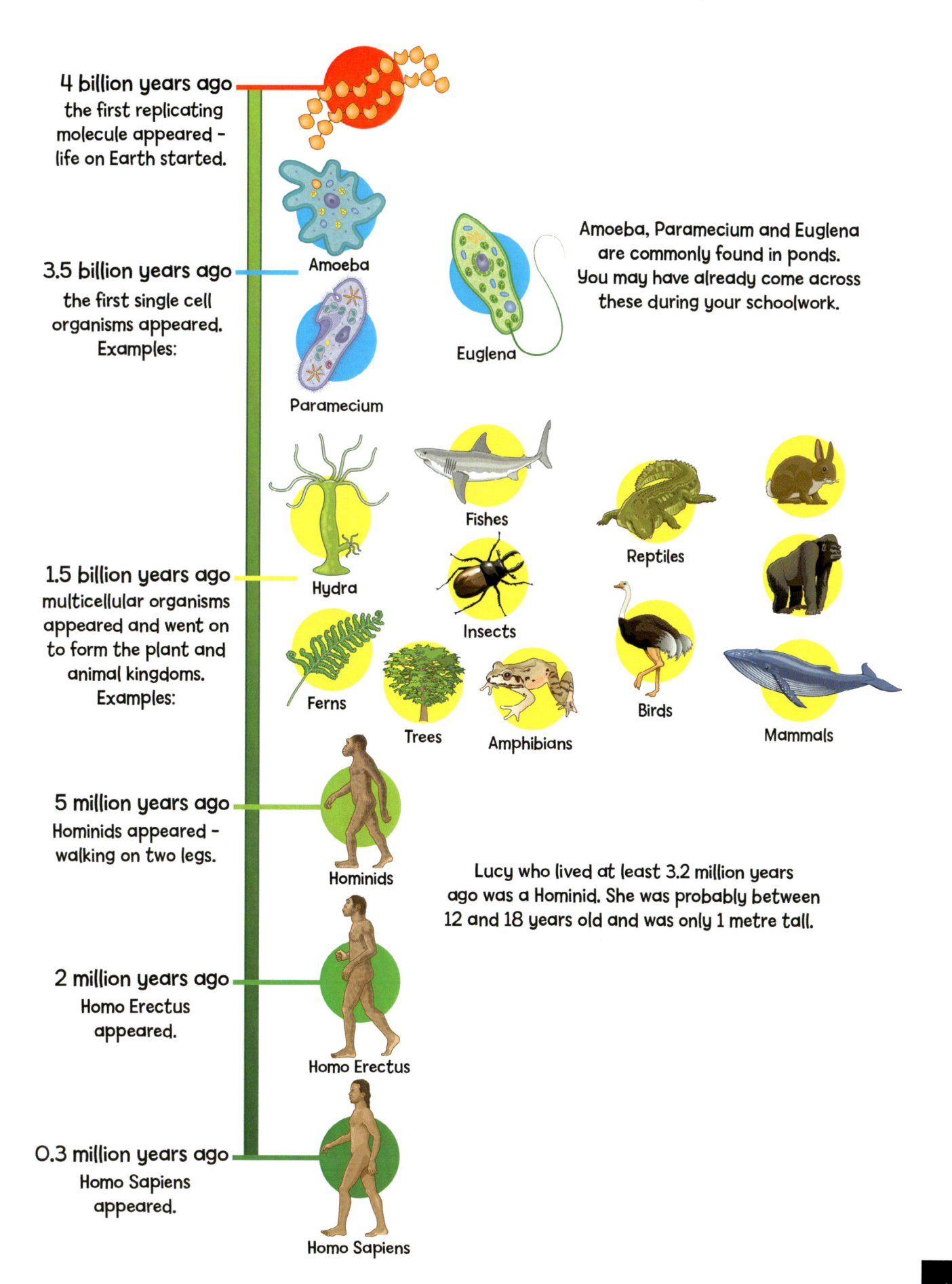

4 billion years ago — the first replicating molecule appeared – life on Earth started.

3.5 billion years ago — the first single cell organisms appeared. Examples:

- Amoeba
- Paramecium
- Euglena

Amoeba, Paramecium and Euglena are commonly found in ponds. You may have already come across these during your schoolwork.

1.5 billion years ago — multicellular organisms appeared and went on to form the plant and animal kingdoms. Examples:

- Hydra
- Ferns
- Fishes
- Insects
- Trees
- Amphibians
- Reptiles
- Birds
- Mammals

5 million years ago — Hominids appeared – walking on two legs.

Lucy who lived at least 3.2 million years ago was a Hominid. She was probably between 12 and 18 years old and was only 1 metre tall.

2 million years ago — Homo Erectus appeared.

0.3 million years ago — Homo Sapiens appeared.

43

To make it easy for you to visualise the timeline of this 4 billion years, image this period to be represented by the average length of a football field – 100 metres (m).

Now, starting at one end of the football pitch, distance 0, where it is 4 billion years ago, walk on to the 12.5 m mark – this is when the single cell organisms appeared.

Walk on to cross over the halfway mark to reach the 62.5 m mark – this is when the multicellular animals appeared and went on to make up all the plant and animal kingdoms.

Continue walking to nearly the very end at the 99.88 m mark to reach the time when Hominids appeared.

Only another 7 centimetres (cm) to get to the 99.95 m mark when Homo Erectus appears.

A further 4 cm on and you reach the 99.99 m mark when Homo Sapiens arrived.

1 cm further and you have arrived at the present time.

Note how very late in the life on Earth timeline we arrived. Out of 100 metres, we arrived at the 99.99 m mark – only 1 cm short of the full span.

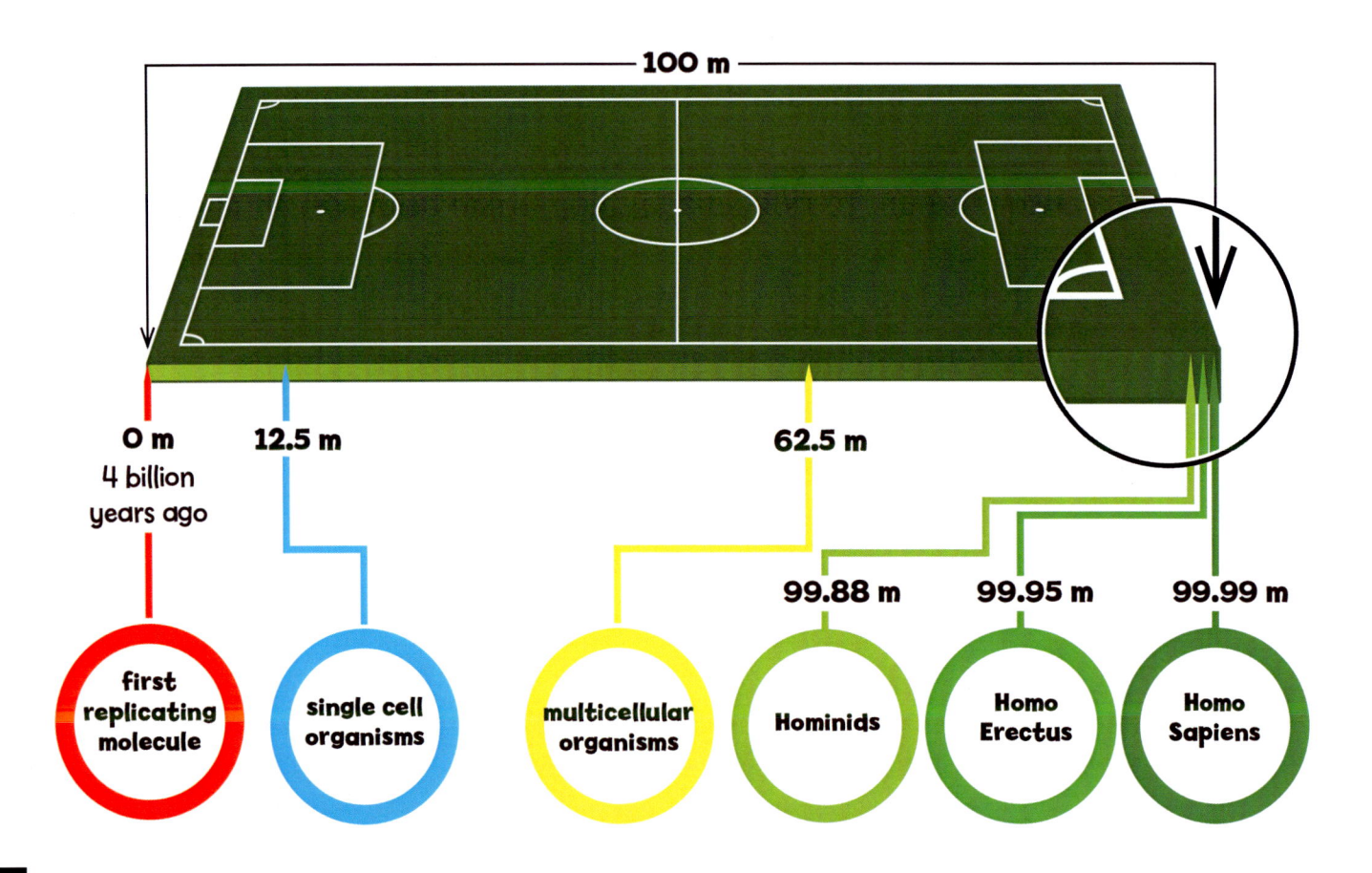

Chapter 6
Modern Humans

Early humans, like their predecessors, were **hunter-gatherers**. They could eat and digest both vegetables and meat which in itself was an advantage. Getting food, by hunting and gathering, like reproduction, became an instinctive behaviour. In many ways it was unfortunate and cruel that they had to kill animals (including humans) to eat and survive, but this has been the path of our evolution. To hunt and to protect themselves against being hunted, humans had to be good fighters, which meant they had to have some aggression in them. They used this to their advantage against other weaker human groups to take what they had to improve their own chances of success and survival. Fights between groups of humans became a way of life and a kind of survival behaviour.

To make sure there was a good supply of food and water all year round, early groups – **tribes** of humans could not stay in one place, and had to travel, often following the rains to find food, like some tribes do today or like the great migration of the wildebeest and zebra in Africa's Serengeti (this word means "endless plains"). This nomadic lifestyle did have some advantages. For example, having to travel made them physically fitter. The women had fewer children, maybe one or two. This meant they had more food to go round, making them healthier.

Climatic changes were frequent and during droughts tribes could no longer rely on following the rains. They needed a constant supply of fresh water and were forced to stay close to rivers. This may have prompted an especially important invention, 12,000 years ago, which was **farming**. Rather than having to move around to find food, clever humans discovered that they could stay put, close to a river, sow seeds and grow their own plants to eat and also feed the animals they had captured and domesticated (by selecting the most docile ones and interbreeding them). There was less need to hunt animals, which was a dangerous thing to do, as sometimes the hunters became the hunted and were injured or killed. As years went by, they became a lot more efficient in producing food. The invention of the **scythe** (tool to cut harvested crops far more easily and quickly) was also a big step forward. They did not need to spend so much of their time farming and were able to use their spare time for other activities and interests, for example specialising in the construction of buildings, engineering and the arts – the beginnings of **professions, higher recreation and culture**. This new set up did have some disadvantages. A change in their diet, eating more sweet vegetables they had grown rather than meat, resulted in terrible tooth decay. They had a constant supply of food, eating whenever they wanted, rather than eating when opportunity arose (which may have been days apart) like their hunter predecessors. There is evidence to suggest that compared to having constantly available food stores to be eaten when required, periods of starvation between meals leads to being healthier even when consuming the same amount of food and calories. The new physically less active lifestyle resulted in much larger families and overcrowding. They often had to live close to domesticated animals for long periods of time. All this prompted the transmission and spread of lethal diseases such as tuberculosis (TB) and smallpox. Nevertheless, this did not stop the relentless and persistent increase in their numbers – the old powerful instinct to replicate and multiply was at it again. Events moved very quickly after this. Towns, then cities and eventually large civilisations appeared. The first big one we know of was the **Sumerian** civilisation which was already well established, only 6000 years ago. It was based in an area of fertile land in between two large rivers, the Tigris and Euphrates. The area, which is in present day Iraq, was called Mesopotamia. This word means "between two rivers". Interestingly, the **wheel** was invented or developed there around 5,500 years ago, during the start of the so-called **Bronze Age**, when humans had made enough progress to move on from the **Stone Age**, to use metals, instead of stones, for making tools and other useful gadgets. The great **Egyptian civilization** was in full swing, around 4000 years ago. It too was based around a huge river, the mighty Nile. Another great civilization was the **Chinese empire**, which arose around 3000 years ago towards the beginning of the **Iron Age**. This was based along the beautiful Yellow River. You may have noticed that in the world today, most cities remain located around rivers. It would be so good to flyby along these great and magnificent rivers and see how they helped humans to flourish and prosper.

These mighty civilisations with their huge collections of people, did have their problems. Just like the earlier smaller groups, these big groups of humans had the urge to explore, expand their territories, and spread but on a much larger scale. One way was to invade and take other nation's territory and belongings. Humans were, instinctively, well adapted to fighting and killing, a legacy from their need to hunt for food to survive. Wars broke out and became a regular, almost a routine event, going on relentlessly and continuing to the present time.

Human intelligence and ingenuity excelled, resulting in some highly significant and important discoveries and inventions that went on to improve and change the way we live. Examples are the discovery of metals such as iron to use for tools and construction; farming (and the scythe) which you already know about; invention of the wheel; more recently the invention of **the printing press**, allowing sharing of information; the **micrometer**, a device designed to measure things accurately and repeatedly, allowing mass manufacture of products; the discovery of modern day **electricity**; invention of the **steam and combustion engines**; the founding of **vaccination**; the discovery of **penicillin**; the discovery of atoms, subatomic particles and electro-magnetic waves and more recently, invention of the telephone, radio, television and, of course computers and the internet which make use of electricity and those magical electro-magnetic waves.

Early humans, like their predecessors, were hunter-gatherers.

Examples of major discoveries and inventions

Farming and the scythe were invented around 12,000 years ago.

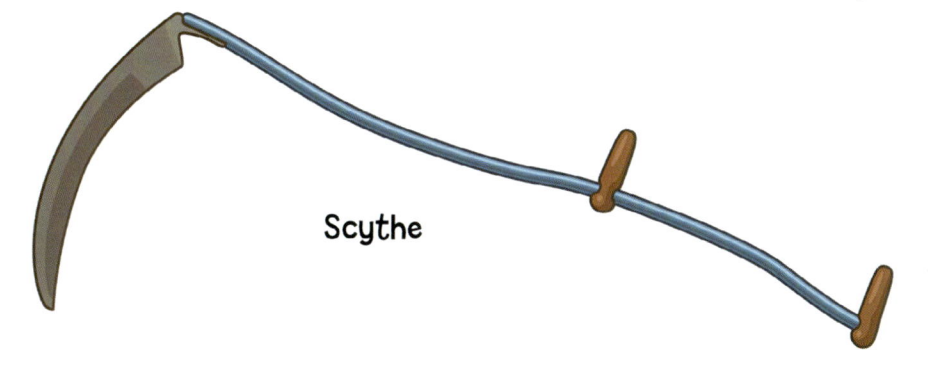

Scythe

The wheel was invented 5,500 years ago in Mesopotamia – present day Iraq.

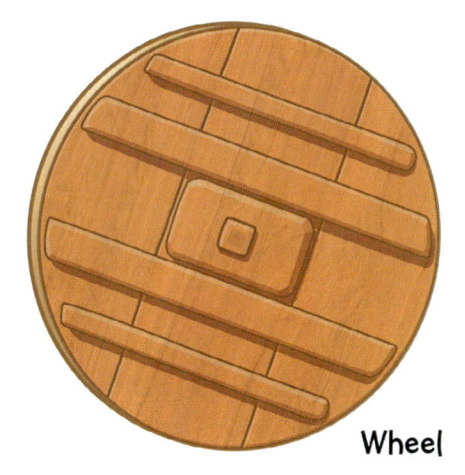

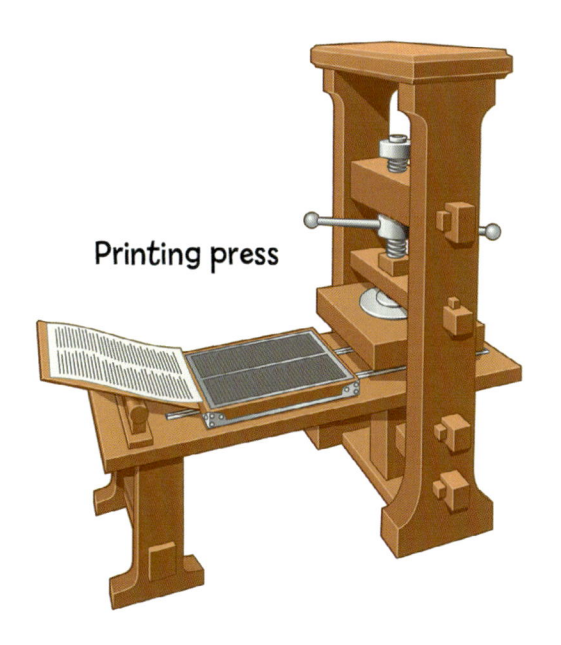

Wheel

Printing press

The printing press which was invented around 1450 – allowed mass distribution of information.

49

The Micrometer, which was invented around 1638 in Leeds in England, allowed accurate and repeated measurements helping to kick start the Industrial Revolution.

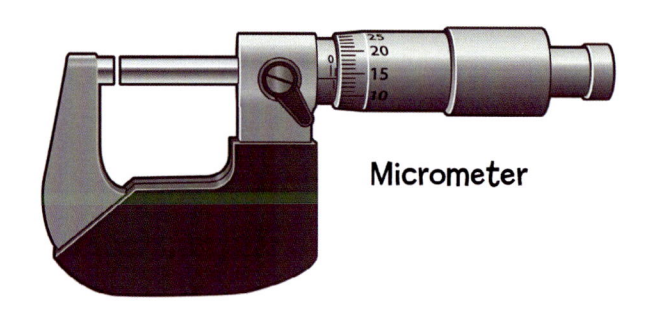

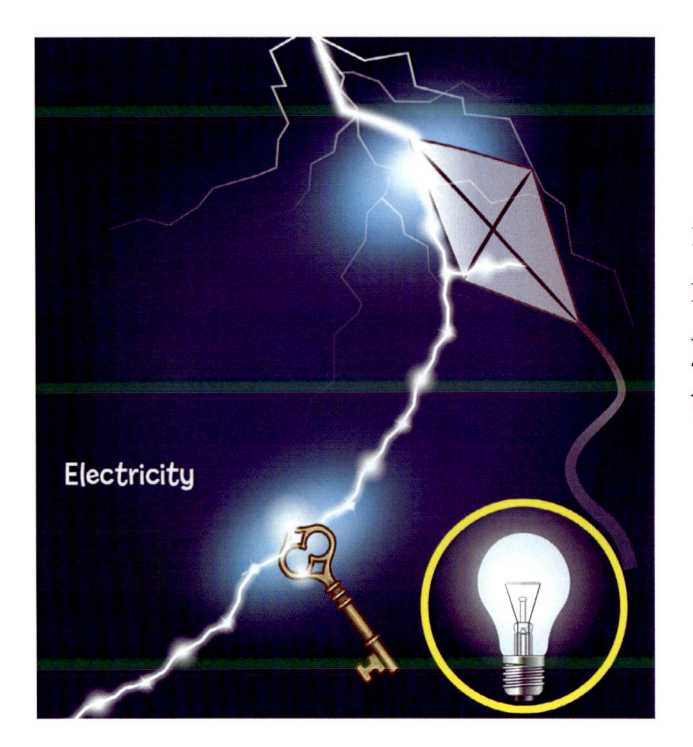

Micrometer

Modern day electricity was discovered in 1752 and went through many modifications over a period of about 140 years, leading on to the development of the alternating current (AC) we use today.

Electricity

Vaccination was founded in 1796, by Edward Jenner and since then has helped to protect huge populations against many diseases.

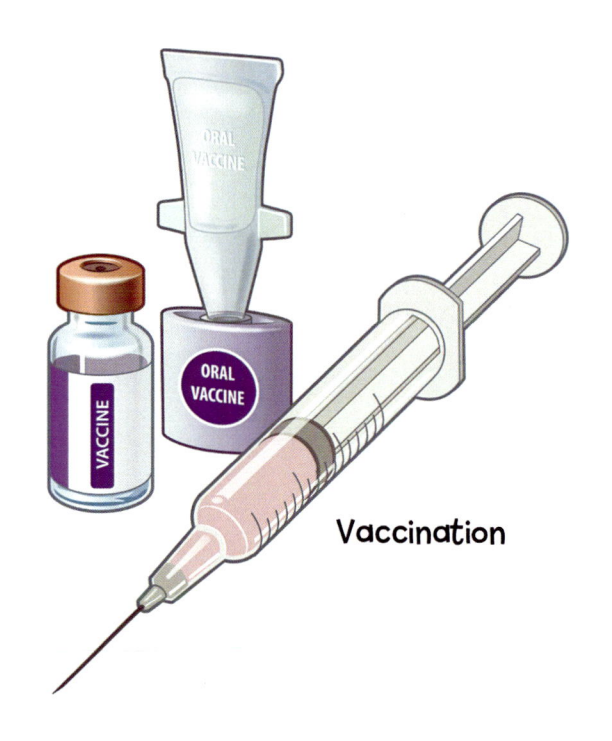

Vaccination

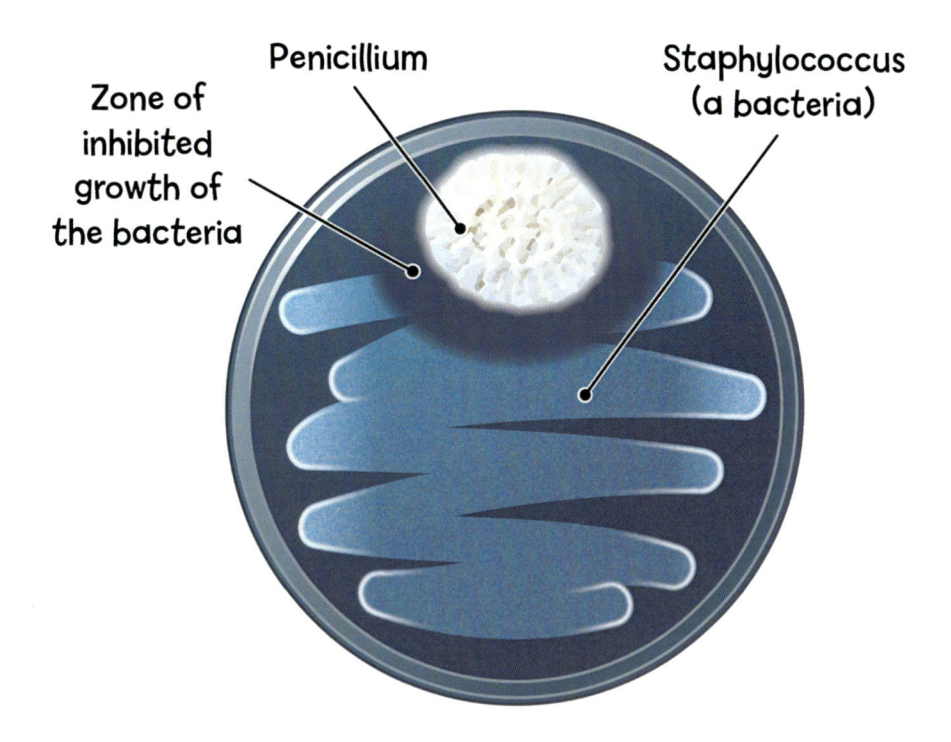

Penicillin, the first antibiotic was discovered in 1928 by Alexander Fleming at St Mary's Hospital in London, who noticed that the mould (a fungus) Penicillium stopped the growth of bacteria. Antibiotics, which kill bacteria, have saved countless lives since then.

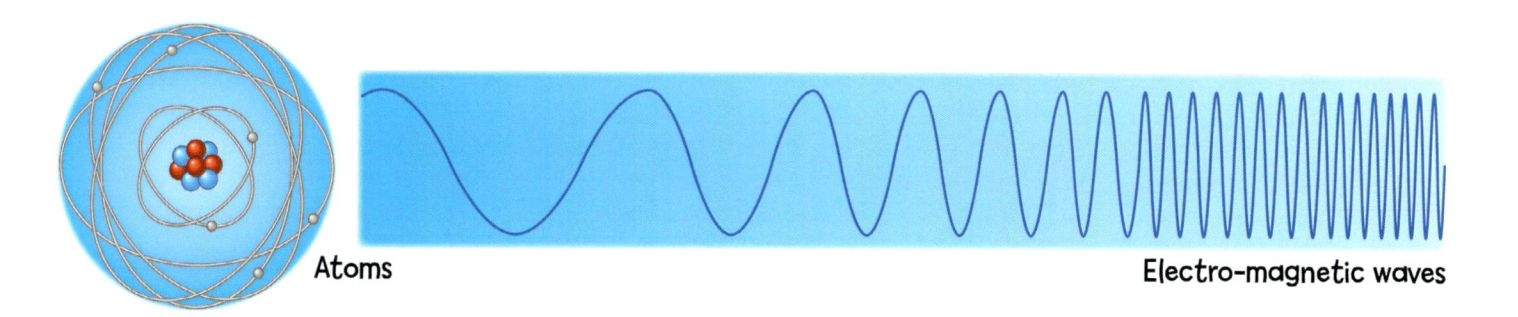

Discovery and understanding of atoms, subatomic particles and electro-magnetic waves dates back to over 200 years and is still progressing.

Invention and construction of the telephone, radio, TV, computers, and the internet over the past 150 years or so, have hugely improved the way we communicate.

Chapter 7
Humans Today and the Near Future

Overall, our behaviour has not really changed much over the past hundreds of thousands of years of evolution. The basic instinct to make "copies" of ourselves – have children – like that first replicator molecule that emerged by chance 4 billion years ago, and was programmed to go on to survive and spread, either as an individual or as a group at the expense of all else, remains well in place. We behave in much the same way, although our intelligence and modern way of life in the civilised world has made some changes to our expected behaviour. To survive, early humans had to hunt and gather. They were instinctively conditioned to continue doing this. It would be reasonable to think that this has now taken the form of shopping and looking for bargains either by searching the shops or by surfing the internet. The instinctive urge to hunt animals is a problem nowadays as for most of us there is no real need to hunt for food and hunting as a sport for pleasure, is disliked by many people. The thing is that this instinctive urge in us, mostly in young men, just like the fighting instinct, is a particularly strong one and needs to be played out and vented otherwise a feeling of frustration or even depression may set in. Maybe we vent these urges by, for example, attending big sports events like football matches, playing video war games and sometimes taking part in violent demonstrations, brawls or even riots. Maybe all these are hunts and tribal warfare being played out today?

As before, we tend to look after those who are genetically, or sometimes geographically, closest to us. In a group, we have a survival advantage. This has persisted over hundreds of thousands of years. The group may be tiny at around a hundred or so, as for example in some tribes in the Amazon forests or may be enormous, as in the countries of India and China running into over a billion. Each group strives to better themselves, which also includes expansion of their territory and imposing or forcing their will over that of other groups. It is not surprising that wars, massacres and genocide have always been part of our history and may well remain so.

In the world today, which has a population of around 8 billion; things are a lot more complex. There is competition amongst individuals as well as between subgroups within a group. It is all driven by the survival instinct. Our intelligent brain, a miraculous and extremely complex organ, does not always function to direct our behaviour as would be expected from an evolutionary point of view. There are big deviations in these "expected" behaviours. Most of these deviations are good ones, for example caring for and looking after humans outside our own groups or looking after and preserving plants and animals (flora and fauna), which have been devastated by the expanding human population, during a relatively very short time. There are also bad deviations, for example within family and within group conflicts, cruelty and killings.

And what of the near future? It is strange that our instinctive urge to replicate and reproduce – which I have mentioned so many times before and I am sorry if you are getting bored with it – may be our downfall. The population of the world is increasing by around 80 million every year. In the past 80 years it has trebled to just less than 8 billion. The resources (everyday things) we use have a limit. Some of us, especially in the richer countries, such as the United States of America and some European countries use at least 6 times more resource, including energy, per person (referred to as people with a **high carbon footprint**) than those in the poorer parts of the world. It may not be long before they catch up with those high users. The world resources cannot cope with such changes. In addition, as I am sure you will all know, our way of life is contributing to other potential setbacks, such as the pollution of our amazing and wonderful planet – the rivers, the oceans and most importantly the atmosphere by treating it as if it was a dustbin and pouring excessive carbon containing gases into it. There is no doubt that this has been a big contributory factor in **climate change** and global warming, which are the current most pressing challenges to us. There have been large fluctuations in our planet's climate in the past, like the ice ages and greenhouse periods, but these had occurred over hundreds of thousands or millions of years. The problem with the current change is the extremely short period in which it is happening. No one doubts that global warming is harmful to all our planet's amazing life forms, which like before may be able to adapt and survive, but with huge changes and costs.

It may be worth mentioning that climate change, pollution and similar challenges are only the symptoms of the underlying problem (the "disease") which remains the relentless and persistent increase in the world population from 2 billion to nearly 8 billion over the last 100 years, resulting in an obvious **overpopulation**. We can blame that first replicator molecule with the unstoppable urge to go on multiplying. Because this urge is such a primitive and forceful thing, it has been difficult to control and stabilise it, despite efforts by many forward-thinking and clever people. However, there is hope, as it seems providing education and reducing poverty also reduces the **birth rate**. It would be so helpful if the major religious leaders of the world, who discourage or forbid contraception and encourage large families, would have a change of heart and advise (but never force) their followers to have smaller families, maybe two or a maximum of three children, especially if the parents are poor and unable to provide for their children to live a full and healthy life. This would have an "immediate" effect, when compared to education and reduction of poverty which may take many generations to achieve. In addition, our scientific advances are beginning to find alternative pollution-free electrical energy sources (such as solar panels, windmill turbines and in the future **nuclear fusion plants**) to recycle materials, and inventing new materials that can be degraded (broken down) by nature, such as bio-degradable plastics.

Increase in human population also increases the chances of diseases spreading throughout the world (**pandemics**) killing many millions as did the "The Black Death" which started 677 years ago (in the year 1346) killing up to 200 million people; "The Spanish flu" which started 105 years ago (in the year 1918) killing up to 100 million people, the "AIDS HIV" infections which started 42 years ago (in the year 1981) killing 3.5 million people up to today and the COVID-19 pandemic which has so far killed around 5 million people. There are also many diseases like malaria and tuberculosis (TB) which are mostly confined to various regions or countries (**epidemic** or **endemic**) and kill millions on a regular basis. These organisms, mostly viruses, that cause these diseases are, just like us and other living things trying to **multiply, survive and spread**. We hate them and have done so well to get rid of them, but can't really blame them, as they are doing the same thing as we are – trying to multiply, survive and spread.

Competition between nations (big groups) and their tendency to expand also increases the chances of world wars, which, if nuclear, may well end human existence. Even if this happens, the planet and most likely many forms of life will survive and flourish, as they did before when 250 million years ago 95% of life on Earth became extinct. Let us be positive and hope our intelligence, ingenuity, common sense and expertise will overcome all these obstacles and we will be OK, for at least the short term.

World Population

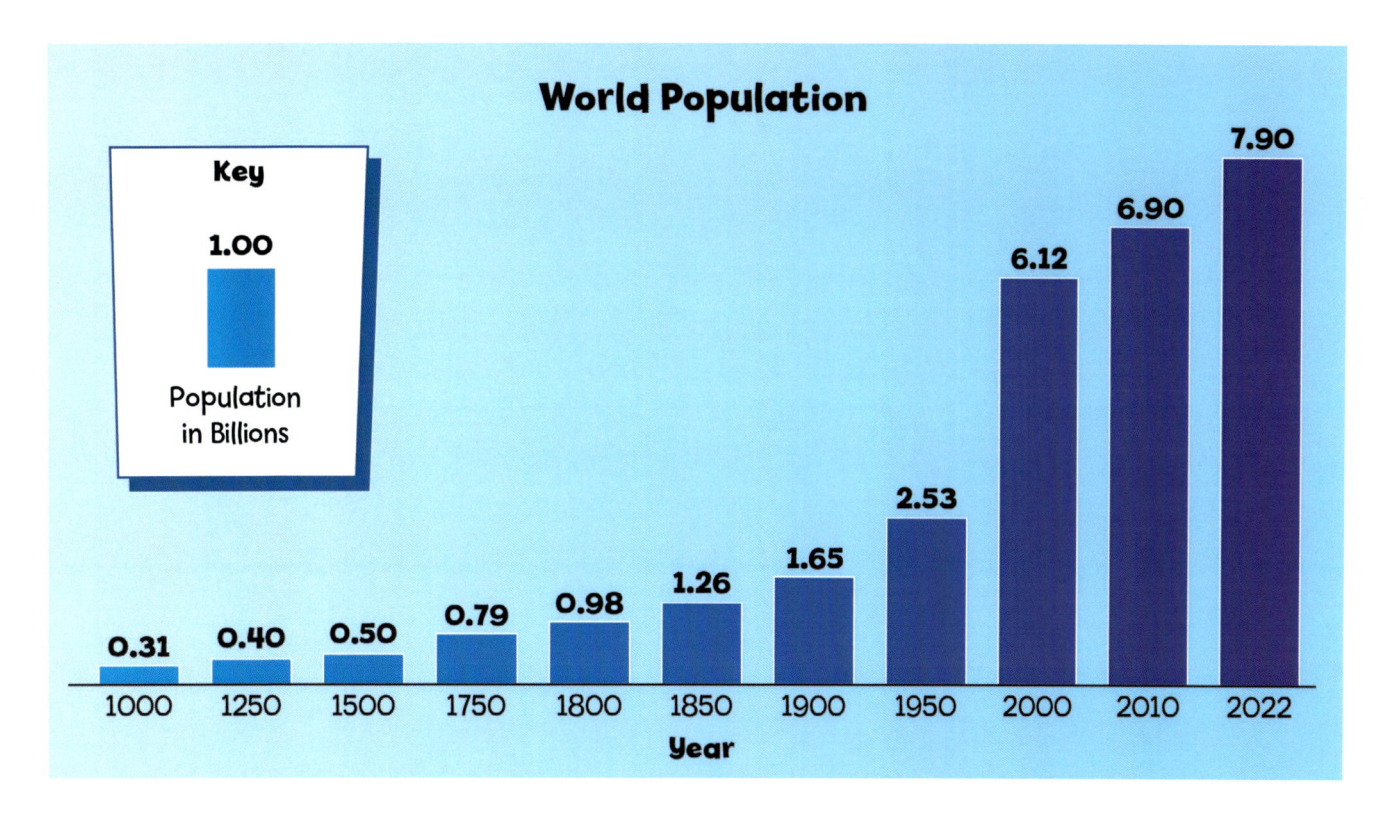

Year	Population (Billions)
1000	0.31
1250	0.40
1500	0.50
1750	0.79
1800	0.98
1850	1.26
1900	1.65
1950	2.53
2000	6.12
2010	6.90
2022	7.90

The overall world population is rising steeply, although the birth rate in wealthier countries may be decreasing. 80 million people are added to the population of the world every year. At the last count, in 2022 the population was 7.9 billion. Around 200,000 people are added to the population every day – that is 9000 per hour and 150 per minute. Not a sustainable situation.

Chapter 8
The Far Future

Your magical giant TV screen has a huge surprise for you. You can flyby on and on to see what the future may hold. Unlike the past all this will be guess work, but you can use your imagination to chop and change things to suit you and make you happy.

Let us assume, with fingers crossed, that humans have done all the right things. Let us assume they have managed to stabilise the world population; recycled the worlds resources, so that they do not run out; have managed to find an energy source that is limitless and non-polluting; stopped climate change and are also looking after all the other life forms – the flora and the fauna. Unfortunately, there are other terrible unexpected things that can happen over which we may not have had a chance to develop technology to control and prevent. Examples are huge sudden volcanic activity which would cut off the sun rays – the Yellowstone National Park in the USA which sits on an old **volcanic caldera** is a likely candidate – or a pandemic against which we have no defence. Far more unlikely would be an asteroid strike like the one that helped to wipe out the dinosaurs 65 million years ago. An even more unlikely example would be the explosion of a nearby dying massive star, a supernova, sending a shower of damaging particles and electro-magnet radiation to Earth which could destroy living things. There was a supernova seen from Earth just over 400 years ago (in 1604), but fortunately it was too far away from us to cause any harm. The next one may be anytime now, or in millions of years – we cannot know.

Possible disasters

Pandemics. Emergence of lethal super contagious viral, bacterial or fungal infections, to which we or animals have no resistance can be a big disaster.

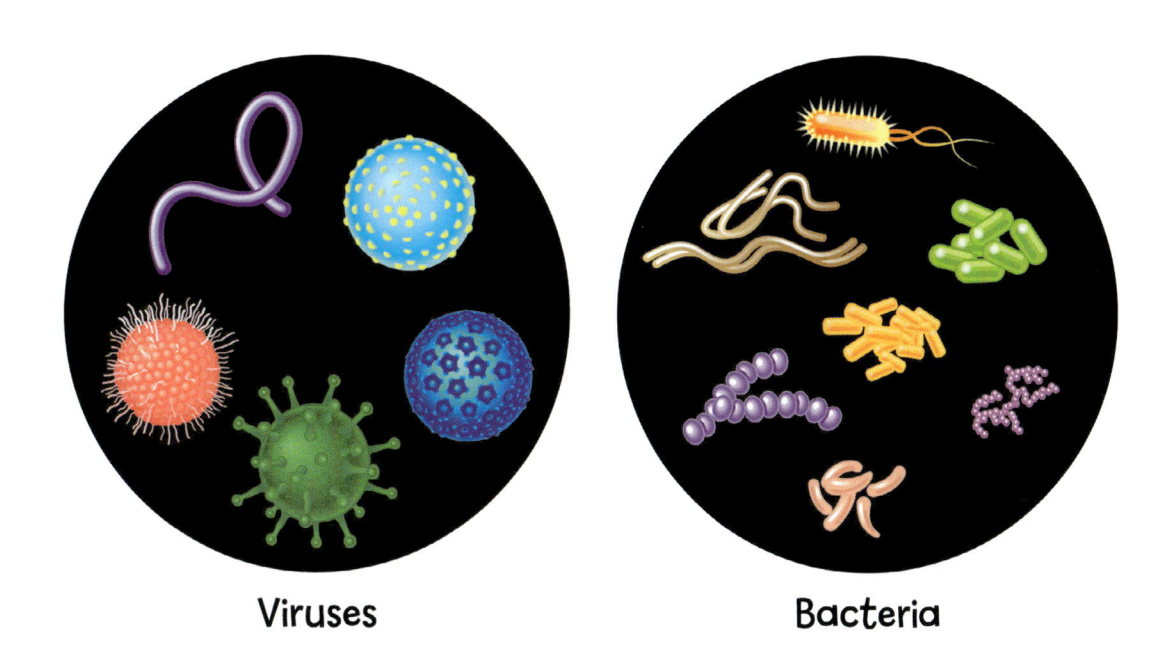

Viruses

Bacteria

A massive volcanic eruption, will result in the blowing up of volcanic material and dust into the atmosphere, blocking the sun followed by the toxic ash raining down – killing many life forms.

Massive volcanic eruption

A massive asteroid hitting our planet could well cause mass extinction of life forms. Even then, maybe some single cell and minute organisms may survive. The asteroid that helped wipe out the dinosaurs and many other animals 65 million years ago, was 12 kilometres in diameter.

If the asteroid strikes land, the dust which will be thrown up into the atmosphere will block the sun destroying life.

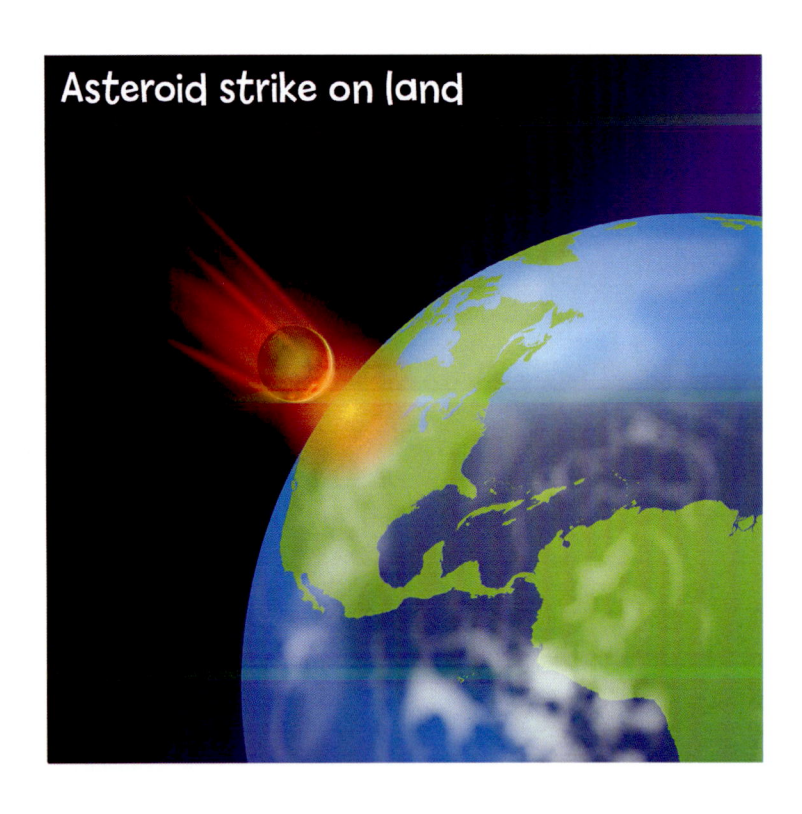

Asteroid strike on land

If it strikes an ocean, then there is the danger of massive water waves (Tsunami) which will flood land masses destroying everything in its path.

Asteroid strike on Ocean

A large star, exploding when it reaches the end of its life, called a supernova, if close enough to us, may kill all life forms, mostly through the high energy gamma (γ) rays, that would reach Earth.

Exploding star

Humans with their ingenuity could well have developed technologies and taken steps to prevent such events destroying life forms. For example, we may have rockets with nuclear warheads to intercept or deviate asteroids heading for Earth or we may have succeeded in travelling into deep space and colonised other planets, to use as a safe place for us to escape to in case of a disaster on Earth. This would also be useful in case the population increase becomes uncontrollable and we need new planets to live on. Ideally, we should find planets with similar size, gravity and conditions to ours, otherwise we would need to change the conditions of these planets to suit us. Perhaps in the far, far future, we would have the knowhow to change our own makeup and chemistry to suit the planet on which we would be planning to live.

There is one certain thing we cannot avoid. In about 5.4 billion years, our life-giving sun will start to run out of hydrogen fuel. It will go on to expand enormously and swallow up and vaporise the whole of the solar system and beyond.

Sun swallows Earth

It is best if we are not on planet Earth just then.

We could have travelled deep into space in enormous space ships and happily settled in many other planets in the infinite known universe.

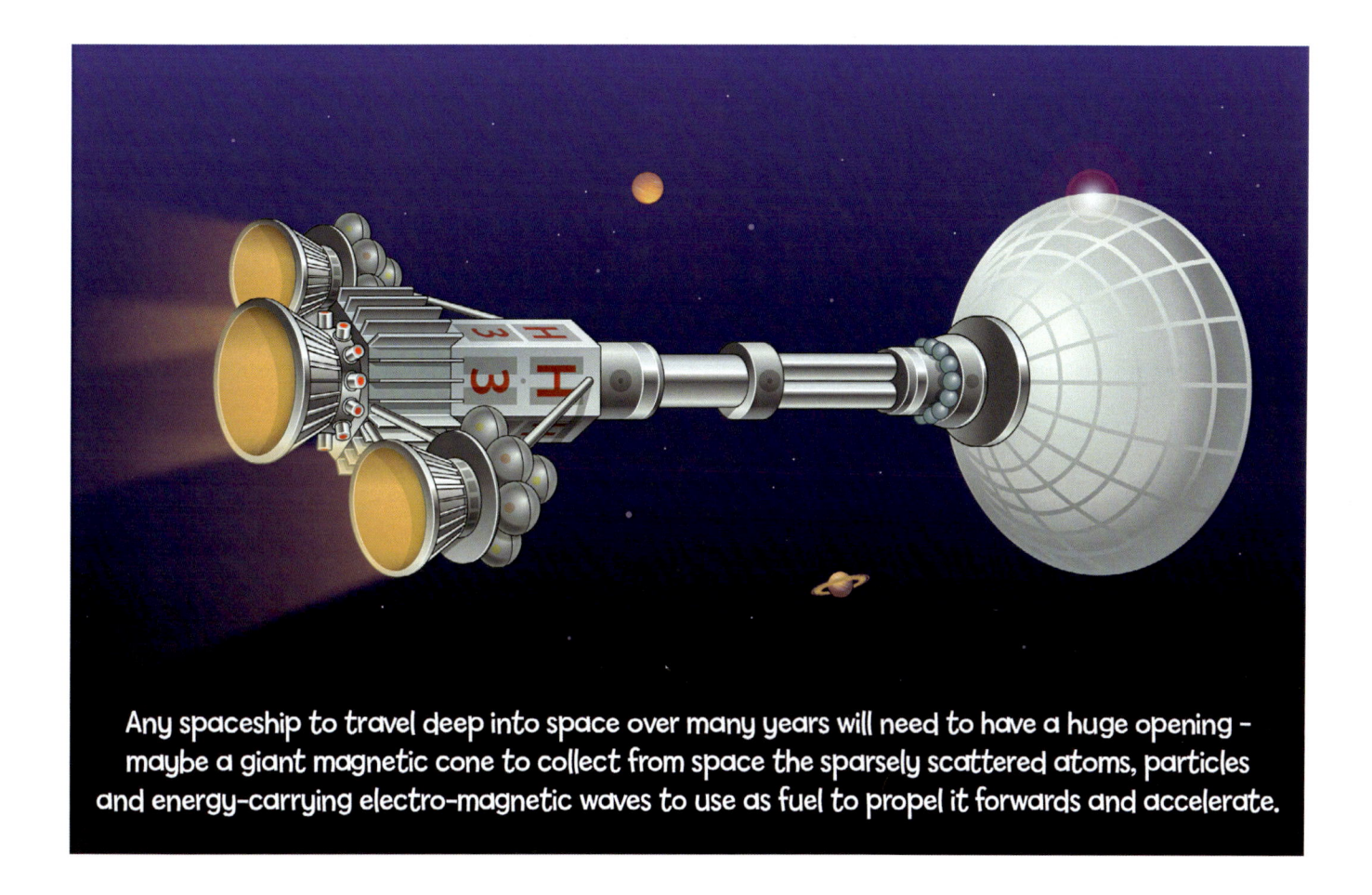

Any spaceship to travel deep into space over many years will need to have a huge opening – maybe a giant magnetic cone to collect from space the sparsely scattered atoms, particles and energy-carrying electro-magnetic waves to use as fuel to propel it forwards and accelerate.

But even then, after at least 10 trillion years the universe would have expanded and cooled to a temperature approaching **absolute zero**, which is -273.15 °C, to have left almost nothing. All the stars and galaxies would have disintegrated and spread out to leave, maybe, just the odd electro-magnetic wave, a few particles or an atom or two whizzing around, with nothing else to bump into – almost back to the very beginning of nothingness when the Big Bang took place.

All these are what the scientists predict will happen. They are not always right – so you can cheer up. Congratulations for persevering to finish reading this book! Now go and treat yourself to an ice cream lolly and then get on with your homework.

Journey's end

Very Cold – almost absolute zero (−273.15°C)

The Magical 3D TV